Behavioral activation theory indicates that much clinically relevant human behavior is a function of positive reinforcement, and that when positive reinforcement is reduced, lost, or chronically low depression results. Behavioral activation encourages clients to obtain and nurture the skills that allow them to establish and maintain contact with diverse, stable sources of positive reinforcement. This creates a life of meaning, value and purpose.

Behavioral Activation: Distinctive Features clarifies the fundamental theoretical and practical features of behavioral activation, integrating various techniques into a unified whole that is efficient and effective. The book includes numerous case examples and transcribed segments from therapy sessions and outlines behavioral concepts using straightforward terms and examples so that all therapists can see the utility and practical value of this approach.

This book will provide essential guidance for students and new therapists, as well as more experienced clinicians wanting to know more about what makes behavioral activation a distinct form of cognitive behavior therapy.

Jonathan W. Kanter is Assistant Professor and Clinic Coordinator at the Department of Psychology, and a Research Scholar at the Center for Addictions and Behavioral Health, University of Wisconsin-Milwaukee.

Andrew M. Busch is currently a pre-doctoral intern at the Alpert Medical School of Brown University and a researcher in the Psychosocial Research Program at Butler Hospital in Providence, Rhode Island.

Laura C. Rusch is an advanced graduate student at the Department of Psychology, University of Wisconsin-Milwaukee.

Cognitive-behavioural therapy (CBT) occupies a central position in the move towards evidence-based practice and is frequently used in the clinical environment. Yet there is no one universal approach to CBT and clinicians speak of first-, second-, and even third-wave approaches.

This series provides straightforward, accessible guides to a number of CBT methods, clarifying the distinctive features of each approach. The series editor, Windy Dryden, successfully brings together experts from each discipline to summarise the 30 main aspects of their approach divided into theoretical and practical features.

The CBT Distinctive Features Series will be essential reading for psychotherapists, counsellors, and psychologists of all orientations who want to learn more about the range of new and developing cognitive-behavioural approaches.

Titles in the series:
Acceptance and Commitment Therapy by Paul Flaxman and
    J.T. Blackledge
Beck's Cognitive Therapy by Frank Wills
Behavioral Activation by Jonathan Kanter, Andrew Busch
    and Laura Rusch
Compassion Focused Therapy by Paul Gilbert
Constructivist Psychotherapy by Robert A. Neimeyer
Dialectical Behaviour Therapy by Michaela Swales and
    Heidi Heard
Metacognitive Therapy by Peter Fisher and Adrian Wells
Mindfulness-Based Cognitive Therapy by Rebecca Crane
Rational Emotive Behaviour Therapy by Windy Dryden
Schema Therapy by Eshkol Rafaeli, David P. Bernstein
and Jeffrey Young

For further information about this series please visit
www.routledgementalhealth.com/cbt-distinctive-features

Behavioral Activation

Distinctive Features

Jonathan W. Kanter, Andrew M. Busch and Laura C. Rusch

Routledge
Taylor & Francis Group

LONDON AND NEW YORK

First published 2009
by Routledge
27 Church Road, Hove, East Sussex BN3 2FA

Simultaneously published in the USA and Canada
by Routledge
270 Madison Avenue, New York, NY 10016

Routledge is an imprint of the Taylor & Francis Group,
an Informa business

Reprinted 2010 (twice)

Typeset in Times by Garfield Morgan,
Swansea, West Glamorgan
Printed and bound in Great Britain by
TJ International Ltd, Padstow, Cornwall
Cover design by Aubergine Creative Design

This publication has been produced with paper manufactured to
strict environmental standards and with pulp derived from
sustainable forests.

British Library Cataloguing in Publication Data
A catalogue record for this book is available from the British Library

Library of Congress Cataloging-in-Publication Data
Kanter, Jonathan.
   Behavioral activation : distinctive features / Jonathan Kanter,
Andrew Busch, and Laura Rusch.
      p. cm.
   Includes bibliographical references and index.
   ISBN 978-0-415-44653-2 (hardback) – ISBN 978-0-415-44654-9
(pbk.) 1. Human behavior. 2. Reinforcement (Psychology) 3.
Behavior therapy. I. Busch, Andrew M. II. Rusch, Laura C. III. Title.
   BF199.K34 2009
   150.19'434–dc22

2008053051

ISBN: 978-0-415-44653-2 (hbk)
ISBN: 978-0-415-44654-9 (pbk)

To Zoe, my primary reinforcer
– JWK

To my parents, for always putting my education
before your new car
– AMB

To Joshua, my husband, who has continually
supported, encouraged, and believed in me
– LCR

"This book gives us new voices in the literature on behavioral activation. It is to be commended for its practicality as well as its well articulated treatment of basic behavioral theory. The authors bring together the principles of BA with important concepts in other newer behavior therapies in a readable and engaging format. *Behavioral Activation* is an outstanding work, and will be a welcomed addition to the libraries of beginning and seasoned clinicians."

Christopher Martell, Private Practice, Seattle; Clinical Associate Professor Department of Psychiatry and Behavioral Sciences and Department of Psychology University of Washington

"All therapists who treat depression should read this excellent overview of behavioural activation. The authors describe an integrated model of depression and a stepped care approach in the application of the behavioural activation. There are good clinical examples and descriptions of how to apply the principles in practice."

David Veale, Institute of Psychiatry, King's College London

Contents

Preface

Behavioral Activation (BA) is an old treatment imbued with a new sense of purpose. Over the last 30 years, at least four empirically supported versions of BA have been developed: Peter Lewinsohn's early version (e.g., Zeiss, Lewinsohn, & Muñoz, 1979), the version incorporated into Cognitive Therapy (CT; Beck, Rush, Shaw, & Emery, 1979) and tested in Jacobson and colleagues' (1996) component analysis, and more recent versions developed by Christopher Martell and colleagues (Martell, Addis, & Jacobson, 2001) and Carl Lejuez and colleagues (Lejuez, Hopko, & Hopko, 2001). These recent versions have generated great interest and excitement, and a wealth of recent, high quality research studies have indicated that BA is a powerful and effective intervention, or set of interventions, for depression. This has sparked even more research and over the next several years we will see an explosion of interest in BA as these results come to light. This convergence of factors led to the inclusion of BA in this current series on the distinctive features of behavioral and cognitive therapies.

All four versions of BA share the common technique of activity scheduling—a very basic technique designed to activate depressed individuals to contact positive reinforcers in the environment. Each version, however, elaborates and adds to this basic technique in different ways, resulting in additional, related techniques, packaged in different ways. Underlying these different techniques are the common threads of behavioral theory and behavioral principles, with each set of techniques based on different aspects of behavioral theory. Supporting these techniques are decades of empirical research.

The glass-half-full view of this situation is that we have a plethora of riches. It is good for clinicians to have options to meet the different needs of clients as well as their own preferences. It is simply more likely that clinicians will be exposed to empirically supported activation techniques if multiple treatments are available and multiple treatment developers are working to disseminate them.

The glass-half-empty view of the situation is that a confusing profusion of activation theories and treatment packages has developed, and there is no overarching theory to guide clinicians in selecting and using specific techniques. Furthermore, multiple and somewhat overlapping sets of techniques may lead to redundant research efforts and slow the process of research. Without an overarching theory that unites and clarifies these techniques, research on BA will suffer and progress will be slowed.

Part 1 of this book will start with basic behavioral principles and theory and build a coherent model of BA that is consistent with the available versions but unifies and clarifies their strengths and areas of emphasis. Part 2 then provides a specific structure for BA treatment that aims to highlight the efficiency and ease of administration of BA techniques, starting with quick, simple and powerful techniques and moving to more complex interventions only as indicated. In this way, the structure capitalizes on BA's strength as a simple approach in the initial sessions, and then capitalizes on BA's strength as an approach that may be functionally tailored to the unique needs and problems of the individual in later sessions. Part 2 outlines each technique in terms of functional application and empirical support, thereby providing the reader not just with an overview of BA techniques but a functional guide to when and how to use them.

The flexible, accessible, and stepped-care nature of Part 2 of this book also describes an approach to implementing BA that is mindful of the pressures of modern outpatient treatment delivery. The average clinician working in the community is often not allowed 20 or more sessions to treat a depressed client, so implementation and progress must occur quickly. Further, most clinicians are not provided with leave time to train adequately in complex treatments, so treatments useful to them must not only be effective, but easy to implement. Within these confines, the community clinician is expected to treat complex, multi-problem clients. These considerations have shaped our writing in the service of making empirically supported treatment for depression available to as many clients as possible.

Throughout the book we emphasize what is distinct about the behavioral theory and the behavioral techniques employed. Thus, the book may be seen as a companion to earlier treatment manuals on BA. However, the current book will also present BA for non-behavioral clinicians and for clinicians who are not familiar with the earlier manuals. Many non-behavioral clinicians are intimidated by behavioral terminology and concepts; this book will outline these concepts in easy-to-understand terms and examples so all clinicians will see their utility and practical value. Thus, it will be useful to a broad range of clinicians. It also may have utility as a training guide for students and student clinicians.

Acknowledgments

We first would like to thank Windy Dryden for the invitation to write this book and Christopher Martell who graciously suggested our names to Windy Dryden.

We would like to acknowledge the community of Behavioral Activation researchers and writers who have supplied the necessary foundational material for this effort, including Peter Lewinsohn, Neil Jacobson, Christopher Martell, Michael Addis, Carl Lejuez, Derek Hopko, and Sona Dimidjian, among many others. A special acknowledgment should go to Christopher Martell for several years of clinical supervision of the first author. Although supervision did not often focus on Behavioral Activation per se, the experience was formative and enduring.

We also would like to acknowledge the developers of three brilliant psychotherapeutic approaches: Functional Analytic Psychotherapy (FAP), Acceptance and Commitment Therapy (ACT), and Dialectical Behavior Therapy (DBT). These master clinicians, specifically Robert Kohlenberg, Mavis Tsai, Steven Hayes, and Marsha Linehan, have been a tremendous influence on the first author (JWK) and their influence is felt throughout this book. In particular we would like to note Robert

Kohlenberg's mentorship and guidance on the basic philosophy and logic of radical behaviorism, how it can be applied to just about anything, and how it can be a model for kindness and compassion.

We would like to thank Joshua Kemp for help with the indexes and our labmates Keri Brown, Rachel Manos, Cristal Weeks, William Bowe, and David Baruch for input on earlier drafts of this manuscript, for myriad contributions to the development of the current approach, and for creating a stimulating and reinforcing lab environment. Finally, we would like to acknowledge Gwynne Kohl—without her sustained, substantial and daily behind-the-scenes efforts and support to the first author this book still would be, perhaps perpetually, in progress.

Part 1

THE DISTINCTIVE THEORETICAL FEATURES OF BEHAVIORAL ACTIVATION

1

A distinctive history

The history of Behavioral Activation (BA) is a true success story. It had its seeds in the early writings of B. F. Skinner (e.g., 1953). Skinner's radical behavioral approach focused scientists and clinicians on environmental factors in depression and how people are sensitive and responsive to their environments. In the early 1970s, prominent behaviorists, trained by and following in the footsteps of Skinner, such as C. B. Ferster and Peter Lewinsohn, elaborated Skinner's writings into a behavioral model of depression. This early theory emphasized the basic behavioral premise that humans are responsive to reinforcement, and when stable sources of positive reinforcement are lost, depression will result. Briefly, Lewinsohn (1974) suggested that, if an individual loses major sources of positive reinforcement, treatment should focus on re-establishing contact with positive reinforcement (activity scheduling), and teaching the skills necessary to obtain and maintain contact with stable sources of positive reinforcement (social skills training).

Dozens of research studies were conducted that were supportive of the basic tenets of this model as well as the corresponding techniques. But with the cognitive revolution well underway by the mid-1980s, progress on the behavioral model had stalled. With the exception of a few hard core behaviorists, behavior therapy for depression came to be seen as inadequate and ill-conceived despite the lack of data to support this view.

The shift to cognitive therapy

What happened? Here we will highlight two prominent events. First, Peter Lewinsohn and his students developed separate treatment manuals for activity scheduling, social skills training, and cognitive restructuring, and compared these three treatment components to a waitlist control condition (Zeiss, Lewinsohn, & Muñoz, 1979). They found that all three treatments performed better than the waitlist control. There were no differences, however, in the effectiveness of the three treatments relative to each other. Lewinsohn concluded from this study that the three treatments should be combined into an integrated cognitive-behavioral treatment approach, which subsequently was published as the self-help book *Control your depression* in 1978 (Lewinsohn, Muñoz, Youngren, & Zeiss, 1978) and the therapy manual *The coping with depression course* in 1984 (Lewinsohn, Antonuccio, Steinmetz-Breckenridge, & Teri, 1984). This marked the end of Lewinsohn's focus on a purely behavioral approach to the treatment of depression.

A second, related event was the ascendance of cognitive approaches to depression treatment, initially fueled by the efforts of pioneers such as Aaron Beck, through his book *Cognitive therapy of depression* (CT; Beck, Rush, Shaw, & Emery, 1979), and Albert Ellis, through his book *Reason and emotion in psychotherapy* (Rational Emotive Behavior Therapy, REBT; Ellis, 1962), as well as many others. Both Beck and Ellis recognized the value of behavioral techniques and incorporated them into their treatments. For example, Beck folded behavioral activation strategies into the original 1979 CT manual, devoting one of its 18 chapters to them. This chapter, Chapter 7, outlined specific techniques for activity scheduling that essentially duplicated Lewinsohn's version of activity scheduling, and suggested that these techniques should be used in the early stages of treatment and specifically with severely depressed clients.

Most importantly, these behavioral techniques were to be used in the context of an overarching cognitive model of depression. Beck and Ellis both suggested that behavioral activation homework assignments were valuable as small experiments designed to challenge underlying assumptions or irrational beliefs. The overall goal became *cognitive* as opposed to *behavioral* change. Thus, while behavioral techniques continued to be employed in cognitive therapy approaches, the underlying behavioral theory upon which those techniques were originally based was lost.

As is often the case in clinical psychology, paradigm shifts are larger than science, as the shift from behavioral to cognitive treatments was not based on scientific findings. In fact, Cuijpers and colleagues (2007) conducted a meta-analysis of 15 studies that had been conducted on behavioral techniques from the 1970s to 1990s, and found that these techniques were very effective for adult outpatient depression compared to waitlist or no treatment controls. Cuijpers and colleagues also found that these techniques were as effective as CT across several studies, and this lack of differential effectiveness extended to follow-up periods as well.

The cognitive therapy component analysis

This subjugation of behavioral techniques to the cognitive model was the final nail in the coffin of a purely behavioral approach to depression for quite some time. Then, in 1996, Neil Jacobson and his colleagues at the University of Washington published a component analysis of CT that resuscitated behavioral techniques. Jacobson and colleagues examined Beck's 1979 CT book and argued that CT could be split into three additive component conditions: (1) activity scheduling (which Jacobson labeled *Behavioral Activation*), (2) a cognitive restructuring condition that included activity scheduling and restructuring automatic thoughts, and (3) the full CT treatment that included activity scheduling, cognitive restructuring, and core belief modification.

Results were quite surprising. Jacobson and colleagues (1996) found no evidence that the full CT package produced better outcomes than the cognitive restructuring or BA conditions, despite a large sample, excellent adherence and competence by clinicians in all conditions, and a clear bias by the study clinicians favoring CT. Also, CT was no more effective than BA at preventing relapse at a 2-year follow-up (Gortner, Gollan, Dobson, & Jacobson, 1998). Jacobson concluded from this study that, because BA was as effective in treating depression as were the other components, this could be taken as evidence that cognitive theory and interventions were unnecessary in the treatment of depression. Simple behavioral activation strategies, he concluded, may be enough.

It may be interesting to compare the Jacobson and colleagues (1996) component analysis study to the Zeiss and colleagues (1979) study described above. Both studies tested several active treatment components against each other, and both found all components to be equally effective. While Lewinsohn interpreted this result as suggesting that the interventions should be combined, Jacobson reasoned, if all interventions are equally effective, why not promote the simplest and easiest-to-train intervention? Why unnecessarily complicate treatment with additional components that, empirically, do not enhance outcomes?

Modern BA

Jacobson and colleagues' (1996) component analysis catalyzed the field and sparked several developments. First, Jacobson and colleagues, not satisfied to refer interested individuals to Chapter 7 of the CT manual, set out to develop a stand-alone BA package, resulting in the book *Depression in context: Strategies for guided action* by Christopher Martell, Michael Addis and Neil Jacobson, published in 2001. In an effort to re-establish a behavioral theoretical foundation for activation techniques, these authors were heavily influenced by the writings of C. B. Ferster (1973), who emphasized the role of avoidance in depression—it is not just that depressed individuals have lost major sources of positive reinforcement, it is also that they may be inactive due to passive avoidance of aversive situations. Thus, the BA techniques described by Martell and colleagues included simple behavioral activation techniques *and* techniques for identifying and overcoming avoidance. The book was written to emphasize the flexible application of treatment techniques rather than presenting a highly structured approach.

Second, Carl Lejuez and his colleagues Derek Hopko and Sandra Hopko developed a different version of BA which they titled *Brief Behavioral Activation Treatment for Depression* (BATD; Lejuez, Hopko, & Hopko, 2001, 2002). They looked to *matching law* (Herrnstein, 1970) for theory, which highlights the importance of looking at the entire context in which behavior occurs, not just at specific reinforcers that follow specific behaviors. Treatment techniques of BATD are highly structured and focused on creating and completing activation assignments, with some additional attention paid to arranging for others in the client's life to effectively support activation. Unlike the Martell version, however, no specific techniques are offered to target avoidance.

Hopko, Lejuez, Ruggiero, and Eifert (2003) have provided an excellent discussion and comparison of BA and BATD. They highlighted that both treatments are much more idiographic than their predecessors, focusing more on how depressed individuals differ from each other in terms of unique environmental situations and histories. Both treatments make an attempt to understand the client's behavior *functionally* and schedule activities based on function, rather than simply scheduling generally pleasant events. Also, both treatments are much more inclusive of factors traditionally seen as non-behavioral, such as biological, genetic, and cognitive variables.

Empirical support

These two alternate versions of Behavioral Activation (which we will call BA and BATD) have generated much interest and empirical support.

First, a major study recently compared BA, CT, paroxetine and a medication placebo (Dimidjian et al., 2006). All treatments performed well for mildly depressed clients, but BA performed surprisingly well for the traditionally difficult to-treat moderately-to-severely depressed clients, outperforming CT and performing equivalently to paroxetine. In addition, paroxetine evidenced a large drop-out rate and problems with relapse and recurrence when the medication was discontinued (Dobson et al., 2004), so BA appears to be the superior treatment in this study when all is considered.

Two other studies of BA have been conducted, including a study supporting a group therapy version of BA in a public mental health setting (Porter, Spates, & Smitham, 2004) and a version of BA adapted for Posttraumatic Stress Disorder (Jakupcak et al., 2006; Mulick & Naugle, 2004). Several other studies are ongoing.

BATD, in turn, has been evaluated through a small randomized controlled trial on an inpatient unit (Hopko, Lejuez, LePage, Hopko, & McNeil, 2003). In this study, BATD produced significantly greater Beck Depression Inventory (BDI) score reductions from pre-treatment to post-treatment compared to general supportive therapy.

The current book

This brief history suggests that there are at least four versions of Behavioral Activation: (1) Lewinsohn's early version, (2) the version incorporated into CT and tested in Jacobson and colleagues' component analysis, (3) the current BA by Martell and colleagues, and (4) BATD by Lejuez and colleagues. The current book aims to unify and clarify the diverse and overlapping set of theoretical positions and clinical techniques that are subsumed under the general label *Behavioral Activation*. In Part 1 of this book, we present the distinctive overarching theory of behavior and depression that guides BA techniques. In Part 2, we outline a unified and clearly articulated set of BA techniques.

2

A distinct definition of human behavior

This Point starts at the very beginning with a simple question: What is behavior? The answer is quite broad—it is everything a person does. Behaviorism has often been viewed as a theory that is most applicable or even only applicable to animals, children, and adults with cognitive disabilities. The modern behavioral theory upon which BA is based, however, allows for the full range of human experience to be relevant to BA.

Traditionally, human psychological functioning has been partitioned into three categories: cognition, affect, and behavior. Modern behavior theory treats all three categories as behavior. Making this shift to an inclusive view of behavior is easy and simply involves changing nouns to verbs. Cognition becomes thinking, affect becomes feeling, and behavior (as traditionally defined) becomes overt acting. According to BA, thinking, feeling and acting are all things people do and thus all can be treated as behavior in any analysis.

To many non-behaviorists, the idea that behaviorists treat private experiences (thinking and feeling) as behavior is puzzling because they were taught that behaviorists deny the existence or relevance of private experiences outright. In fact modern behavioral theory seeks to explain private experiences of all types, including thinking, feeling, loving, dreaming, wishing, remembering, and even the experience of self (Kohlenberg and Tsai, 1991). Modern behavioral theory takes into account the whole range of human experiences. The key difference between the behavioral view and most other schools of thought in psychology is that these private experiences are seen as private behaviors, not the causes of behaviors. Private and public behaviors differ in terms of scale and accessibility, in that private behaviors may be very subtle and only observable to the person engaging in the behavior. But, private behaviors can be accounted for with the same learning principles and change processes as can public behaviors.

While behaviorists do not deny the existence of private behaviors, they do object to substituting mental entities for private behaviors, and then using these entities to explain the behaviors. Examples of this are quite prevalent. We remember well (behavior, verb) because we have a good memory (noun, mental entity). We act intelligently (behavior, verb) because we have high intelligence (noun, mental entity). We think in certain ways (behavior, verb) because of our schemas (noun, mental entity). Behaviorists refer to such mental entities as *explanatory fictions*. To a behaviorist, the concepts of memory, intelligence, and schemas ultimately are circular, do not explain much at all and obscure the search for more useful causes. If you acted intelligently because of your intelligence, what have we learned about you, other than that you act intelligently? If you remembered something because of your good memory, what have we learned, other than that you remember things well? We now need another set of analyses to understand the factors that cause high intelligence and good memory. Thus, behaviorists instead seek to understand the current and historical variables that lead individuals to engage in the behaviors of remembering, acting intelligently, and thinking about specific things. It is ultimately believed that this analysis will be useful for designing interventions to help people remember more accurately, act more intelligently, and so forth.

From the behavioral view, clinical psychology is rife with explanatory fictions purported as the causes of behavior. Examples include schemas, personality, and self-esteem. Diagnostic labels can also function as explanatory fictions: "She acts that way because she has Borderline Personality Disorder." Diagnoses are important, helpful in communicating with other professionals, and often useful when linked with empirically supported treatment techniques, but they often provide no additional useful information in terms of causes or etiology and, thus, are not emphasized in behavioral analyses.

Flexible units of analysis

A final point to make is that modern behavioral theory allows for very flexible definitions of behavior. Any behavior can always be compartmentalized into smaller behaviors. For example, one may go for a walk, and that behavior may be defined as the unit that encompasses getting up from one's chair, moving to the door, opening it, going outside, walking around the block, and returning inside. The entire "walk" is the behavior of interest. Alternately, each of those components may be defined as the behavior of interest (e.g., getting up from one's chair or opening the door). At an even more molecular level, those behaviors in turn can be compartmentalized. Opening the door, for example, involves moving one's arm, grasping the door handle, turning it, and pushing on it. This can go on and on into infinitely smaller units of analysis.

The important point is that there is no "right" unit of analysis. Because behaviorism is a pragmatic system, the behavioral units of analysis are defined in terms of what is useful clinically. Thus, loving, trusting, escaping, cheating, avoiding, sleeping, having an argument, studying for a test, hoping, and so forth, may all be considered behaviorally. The language of the client, rather than technical behavioral language, is preferred, although certainly the clinician may help clarify the focus of the language to make sure it is useful. The behavior of the whole human organism, broadly defined, using the language of the client, is the focus of the analysis.

3

Distinct terminology

BA employs a distinctly behavioral terminology, with which many readers may be unfamiliar. Thus, this Point defines some basic terms that will be used and described in more detail throughout this book. These definitions are not intended to be technical descriptions, but rather to provide an understanding at a level that will facilitate clinical work and increase the usefulness of the remainder of this book. The list below may serve as a reference that can be returned to when tripped up at any point by behavioral terminology.

Operant behavior

Operant behavior is behavior controlled by both the current and historical context. In terms of the current context, operant behavior requires *discriminative stimuli* to evoke the behavior. In terms of the historical context, operant behavior has been shaped by consequences that have followed the behavior in the past. These consequences include *positive reinforcement*, *negative reinforcement*, and *punishment*. To fully describe a particular example of an operant behavior, the discriminative stimuli that evoked the behavior and the consequences that followed it in the past should be described. Together, the discriminative stimuli, behavior, and consequences make up a *contingency* or *contingent relation*.

Most complex clinically relevant human behavior can be conceptualized as operant behavior. Operant behavior has a voluntary, goal-directed feel to it, such as walking, planning, cleaning, eating, talking, dancing, writing, and so on. Operant behavior is at the heart of this book, because Behavioral Activation ultimately aims to activate the operant behavior of clients.

Positive reinforcement

Positive reinforcement is said to occur when the introduction of any stimulus following a given behavior increases the frequency of that behavior in the future. For example, a shy person may begin going to more social events if an initial outing results in positive social interactions. In this case, the positive social interactions functioned as positive reinforcers, making going to social events more likely. Positive reinforcers may include rewards, such as tokens or praise, naturally occurring reinforcers, such as food and sunlight, mechanical operations, such as a car starting or door opening, and social reinforcers. Behavioral activation seeks to increase contact with diverse and stable sources of positive reinforcement.

Negative reinforcement

Negative reinforcement is said to occur when the removal or avoidance of any stimulus following a given behavior increases the frequency of that behavior in the future. For example, long-term drug use is often described as maintained by negative reinforcement in that the behavior of taking the drug results in the removal of withdrawal symptoms. For an individual with chronic pain, the behavior of staying in bed is negatively reinforced by avoidance of increased pain. The removal of withdrawal symptoms and avoidance of increased pain make the behaviors that produced these consequences more likely to occur in the future. A key process to BA, *experiential avoidance*, is behavior negatively reinforced by the removal or reduction of aversive emotional experiences.

Punishment

Punishment is said to occur when the introduction of any stimulus following a given behavior decreases the frequency of that behavior in the future. For example, if smoking behavior decreases when it is reliably followed by complaints from a partner, one would say that complaining is punishing. If the removal or avoidance of a stimulus reliably increases the rate of the behavior that preceded it (negative reinforcement) or its introduction leads to a decrease in behavior (punishment) it generally can be referred to as an *aversive stimulus*.

Discriminative stimuli

Operant behavior is said to be *evoked* by *discriminative stimuli* or aspects of the environment that signal that a given consequence is possible. For example, a phone ringing is a discriminative stimulus for the behavior of answering the phone. In BA, it is important to assess discriminative stimuli for positive operant behavior, to make sure that the prompts for positive behavior are available in the environment.

Extinction

Extinction is said to occur when the frequency of a behavior decreases after the consequence for that behavior is withdrawn. Extinction is important to the behavioral model of depression, as will be discussed, because the reductions in behavior seen in depression sometimes may be viewed as resulting from withdrawal of positive reinforcers. In other words, healthy, non-depressed behavior has been extinguished.

Respondent behavior

Respondent behavior is behavior that is simply generated automatically by certain stimuli, known as *eliciting stimuli*.

Eliciting stimuli can be unconditioned (stimuli that elicit natural, reflexive responses, such as startle and fear in response to a loud, unpredictable noise) or conditioned (stimuli that elicit certain responses only because they have been paired with unconditioned stimuli in the past, such as startle in response to seeing the individual who has been making loud, unpredictable noises). Respondent behavior is simpler than operant behavior and often has more of a reflexive, physiological feel to it. Many of the emotional reactions seen in depression are conceptualized as respondent behavior, automatically elicited by negative environmental events.

Many other terms could have been defined here and we make no claim to have created an exhaustive list. Becoming a competent BA clinician, however, does not require years of study of behavioral terminology. The current list should be sufficient. Most important is the ability to think *functionally*, a topic we turn to in the next Point.

4

A distinct philosophy and theory

The scientific philosophy upon which BA techniques are based has evolved from early writings on *radical behaviorism* by B. F. Skinner (1953, 1974) to *functional contextualism* by Steve Hayes (Gifford and Hayes, 1999; Hayes, 1993; Hayes, Hayes, Reese, & Sarbin, 1988). In developing *functional contextualism*, Hayes in essence critically evaluated the scientific philosophy of radical behaviorism advanced by Skinner, which had been very successful as a framework for basic non-human behavioral research and applied behavioral interventions in controlled settings (e.g., residential settings), but less successful as a framework for the development of interventions for adult, outpatient populations. Hayes clarified, elaborated, reformulated, and repackaged the important themes from this early philosophical system, stripping away some of the jarring and polemical aspects of Skinner's work and distilling the core elements that are important to adult, outpatient populations. BA may be seen as based on functional contextualism, but some behaviorists may instead consider it a radical behavioral, or behavior-analytic, approach.

Context and meaning

To a behaviorist, to understand the meaning of a behavior we must understand its function. To understand the function, we must understand the specific current and historical variables that lead the individual to engage in the behavior. We ask, how does a behavior affect the environment? What is a behavior in the service of? What will the behavior produce (i.e., positive reinforcement) or remove (i.e., negative reinforcement)?

A focus on the historical context and function

It is very easy to misunderstand what is meant by *function* at this point, because most of us believe that we engage in behavior because we *want* a certain consequence to happen. But such *wants*, *needs*, or *intentions*, from a behavioral perspective, are examples of private behaviors that can easily become explanatory fictions. To be absolutely clear, we are not denying that people engage in behaviors that usefully can be described as wanting, needing or intending, we are just suggesting that wants, needs, and intentions are not usefully construed as ultimate causes, because we are still left with the task of identifying why an individual wanted or needed something. Any parent who, after asking a child why he or she engaged in a certain behavior, receives the response, "Because I wanted to," understands the futility of such an analysis. An analysis that ends with the identification of a want or related private experience has ended prematurely if the goal is to intervene successfully on the behavior of interest.

The language of wanting, needing, and intending also has the effect of moving the analysis into the future. It suggests that we engage in a certain behavior because we want a certain consequence to occur *in the future*. A basic principle of behavior, however, is that a behavior's function is determined by the consequences that have followed a behavior *in the past*. We drink a cup of water, not because doing so *will result* in the quenching of thirst, but because doing so *has resulted* in the quenching of thirst in the past.

Ask yourself this question: Would you pick up that glass of water and drink it, if, in the past, doing so had never resulted in the quenching of thirst? Of course not. Focusing on past contingencies is tricky for most individuals because it runs somewhat counter to actual experience. In the moment, we are in contact with the experience of wanting to drink, and not with the past contingencies that have successfully reinforced drinking, but that does not mean that the past contingencies are not the important, controlling variables from a scientific, causal perspective. Behaviorists often refer to a *reinforcement history* which is the sum total of past contingencies that have shaped a behavior and account for why it is likely to occur in the future.

A focus on the current context

In addition to understanding the reinforcement history, we also must understand the current context. This is much easier to appreciate, because the current context is, indeed, current and therefore more available to the individual engaging in the behavior. For example, the presence of a cup of water is a necessary feature of the current context for the behavior of drinking a cup of water to occur. The *wanting* of a drink of water (or the experience of thirst, or, more technically, a recent history of water deprivation, but that is beyond the scope of this Point) is also important and may be considered an additional necessary feature of the current context (but not an ultimate cause). Other more subtle variables may also be important (e.g., is the water in the glass very cloudy and unhealthy looking?). In total, these current contextual stimuli that are necessary for the behavior to occur are termed *discriminative stimuli.*

So far, we have been discussing *operant behavior*, which is behavior that is evoked by discriminative stimuli in the current context and that has been followed by reinforcing stimuli in the historical context. Operant behavior has a voluntary, goal-directed feel to it. Most complex clinically relevant human behavior can be conceptualized as operant behavior. In fact, the goal of BA is to activate a broad class of operant behaviors that result in contact with positive reinforcement, from simple behaviors such as getting out of bed to complex behaviors such as negotiating for a raise.

Respondent behavior

Many non-behaviorists have confused the theory of operant behavior with a *stimulus-response* behaviorism that focuses entirely on the current context and ignores the role of reinforcement history. There is a way the current context can generate behavior in the absence of a reinforcement history, but we are no longer talking about operant behavior. Some behavior is simply generated automatically by certain stimuli, and this is known as *respondent behavior*. Many readers undoubtedly are familiar with Pavlov's dogs, the seminal example of respondent behavior: Food pellets provided to the dogs automatically elicited the behavior of salivation, and, over time, through respondent conditioning (also called classical conditioning), stimuli paired with the food pellets (e.g., a bell) also came to elicit the salivation.

Respondent behavior is different from operant behavior in that it is simpler and often has more of a reflexive, physiological feel to it. Clinically, displays of emotion, such as crying, sadness, anger, and excitement, often are respondent (at least partially). It is clear that these "basic" emotions have a hereditary basis and are elicited automatically in specific situations. It is also clear, however, that the adult expression of emotions is a complex learned experience—an elaboration of these basic automatically elicited emotions.

It is important for the BA clinician to distinguish respondent emotional displays from operant emotional displays. Consider a client who starts crying in session in response to a clinician's question, "How was your week?" On the one hand, this could be respondent behavior, in that the question put the client in contact with some very upsetting events that happened during the week, and this automatically elicited sadness and tears. But the crying could also have an operant function, in that crying has been positively reinforced by its production of sympathy, caring and gentleness from others, including the clinician, in the past. The crying, in essence, may function as avoidance, with the client telling the clinician, "Treat me nicely this week, and do not push me too hard." It is important to understand, however, that even if the crying has such an operant function, the client is not necessarily doing it on purpose, consciously, or manipulatively. The clinician may feel manipulated but this does not mean the client is purposely being manipulative. Such is the nature of operant behavior (Linehan, 1993). Of course, multiple respondent and operant functions of a single behavior are probable. Human behavior is complex.

A focus on function versus form

Behavior defined by its function needs to be contrasted with behavior defined by its form. Behaviors that look similar may have different functions. As mentioned above, crying may function to produce escape from an unpleasant interaction, or it may function to evoke pity and sympathy from others. The function will depend on who is present during the crying (the discriminative stimuli) and how similar individuals have responded to crying in the past (the reinforcement history). Telling jokes with friends may function to elicit social reinforcement (e.g., laughter from friends), but telling jokes at a funeral may function as a way to distance oneself from sadness or grief. Again, the key is the historical and current context. In the absence of any knowledge of the historical and current context, crying and telling jokes are incomprehensible behaviors.

A hopeful determinism

The language of modern behavioral theory has the potential to elicit a certain hopelessness, in that, if behavior is simply a product of our pasts and our environments, it is out of our control and there is nothing we can do to change it. The determinism of modern behavioral theory, however, is hopeful in that clients can be empowered to change their environments, thereby creating a new history that over time will generate new and more functional behavior. BA presents a set of techniques designed to do just that. According to BA, clients' problems may indeed be products of their histories and their environments, but that does not mean there is nothing that can be done to change things for the better. Put this way, modern behavioral theory is both non-blaming and empowering. This is often a helpful therapeutic stance as it creates empathy for clients and their struggles, but also focuses the clinician on helping the client take action, even in the face of seemingly overwhelming histories.

5

The distinct behavioral ABC model

The previous Point highlighted that most complex, clinically relevant human behavior is operant in nature. To fully understand operant behavior, one must understand its function. This involves specifying, as precisely as possible, the current context that evokes the behavior, the form of the behavior itself, and the historical context that has reinforced the behavior. The process of specifying these three components of operant behavior is termed *functional analysis*, or, more loosely, *functional assessment*. To make functional analysis simple for clinicians, modern behavioral theory employs a distinct ABC model.

The ABCs of behavioral theory

In the behavioral ABC model, "A" represents the antecedents for the behavior (discriminative stimuli in the current context that evoke the behavior), "B" represents the behavior, and "C" represents the consequences (reinforcing or punishing stimuli that have followed the behavior in the historical context). Ramnerö and Törneke (2008, p. 48) summarize the model succinctly with three simple questions:

- Behavior (B): What is the person doing?
- Antecedent (A): When does the person do it? The question "When?" is meant broadly, more like, "In the presence of what does the person do it?"
- Consequence (C): What happens immediately after the person does it?

Figure 1 shows how the behavioral ABC model is both similar and different from the traditional cognitive ABC model (newer

Theory	A	B	C
Cognitive	Antecedent (invited to social event, anxious)	Belief ("I am a loser")	Consequence: Affective or behavioral (more depressed, stays at home)
Behavioral	Antecedent (invited to social event, anxious)	Behavior (stays at home)	Consequence: Function (reduced anxiety)

Figure 1 Comparison of the ABCs according to cognitive and behavioral theory

cognitive models emphasize cognitive processes to a greater degree, while the traditional model described here emphasizes cognitive content). First, the antecedents are basically the same. For example, a depressed client, Joe, is invited to a social event and becomes anxious at the prospect of attending. The combination of an event and a private experience may be seen as the antecedent in both models. Traditionally, such private events are not thought of as antecedents in the behavioral model, instead focusing on environmental events, but there is little harm in loosening this stance and also considering thoughts and feelings as antecedents if it is useful clinically to do so. In other words, in behavioral theory the ultimate cause is environmental but, if the environmental antecedents are very distant, unclear, or unalterable, it may be clinically useful to include thoughts and feelings. Feelings are typically antecedents in BA, especially, as is seen here, when reductions in that feeling also serve as consequences that maintain avoidance behavior.

In both models, "B" represents the variable that is targeted for change. In cognitive theory, the target is the belief—in this example, "I am a loser." In behavioral theory, it is the behavior—in this example, the behavior of staying at home and

not going to the party. Cognitive processes may also be construed as behavior in this model, such as ruminating, worrying,
criticizing one's self, or thinking about suicide. The focus,
however, is on the consequences of this behavior, not the
content per se.

In both models, "C" represents the relevant consequence but
what consequence is relevant is different for each model.
Cognitive theory focuses on potential affective or behavioral
consequences that result from reacting to antecedents with
specific beliefs. Thus, the client is taught to see how holding the
belief "I am a loser" unchallenged leads to increased depression
as well as the behavior of staying at home and not going to the
party. Behavioral theory focuses on consequences that may
function to maintain and strengthen the behavior of not going
to the social event. In this case, staying at home results in
successful termination of the anxiety that was elicited by the
prospect of attending the social event, making the behavior
stronger and more likely to occur in similar situations in the
future (negative reinforcement). In sum, cognitive theory
attempts to identify the specific affective or behavioral consequences of specific beliefs in specific situations, in order to help
the client change the beliefs to produce different consequences.
Behavioral theory attempts to identify problematic Antecedent-
Behavior-Consequence relations and to potentially manipulate
all three variables.

Several additional examples of the behavioral ABC model
may be helpful at this point:

• Consider Sarah who, like Joe, is depressed and socially
  anxious but, unlike Joe, actually goes to a social event (A).
  At the event, Sarah stays seated on the couch, making little
  effort to socialize (B). This behavior may avoid the stress of
  social interaction temporarily (C), and functionally may be
  equivalent to not going to the social event at all. Both not
  going to a social event and being unsocial at a social event
  can be categorized together as topographically different

forms of avoidance behavior. Similarly, Sarah may leave the event early (B), thereby escaping the stress experienced at it (C), demonstrating another form of avoidance. Both of these consequences negatively reinforce the corresponding behaviors of limited socializing and leaving the event early.

- Terry has to complete his taxes; it is now approaching mid-April and he is experiencing increased anxiety and stress (A). In response Terry spends several hours organizing and reorganizing the paperwork but does not actively start completing the forms (B). Such behavior also may be considered avoidance to the degree that it successfully temporarily reduces the stress associated with doing taxes, because the individual is, after all, doing something (or so he may convince himself), but also successfully avoids the anxiety and stress that would occur if he actually tried to complete the forms (C). Again, the behavior here is negatively reinforced.

- Consider Patrick who is experiencing depression, is struggling with work and has received negative feedback from a supervisor (A). That evening, Patrick complains to his wife about work, how overwhelmed he feels, and how tired of it he is (B). His wife listens intently, offers sympathy and support, and—although usually they do this together—makes dinner and cleans up afterwards (C). Inadvertently, and trying to be helpful, Patrick's wife may have reinforced complaining, making it more likely Patrick will do so in the future. Patrick's wife's sympathy, support and extra effort to be nice have positively reinforced Patrick's complaining. In this case, intervention must be sensitive. We do not want spouses to become unsympathetic in BA, but we do encourage expressions of sympathy that do not reinforce depressive behavior.

A final point to make is that a behavior or consequence in one contingency can be an antecedent in the next. Antecedents, behavior, and consequences can only be broken up for purposes of analysis. In reality, we are talking about a steady, inter related and overlapping stream of functional relations. Consider the example above of Patrick and his wife. While his wife may have reinforced Patrick's complaining by doing the dishes, Patrick's behavior of complaining, in turn, becomes the antecedent for his wife's behavior of doing the dishes and cleaning up, which may be negatively reinforced by an immediate reduction in Patrick's complaining. What neither Patrick nor his wife realize, however, is that they are caught in a cycle that is maintained by immediate consequences. Over time the contingencies may be strengthened and the problems may become more entrenched.

How to conduct functional assessment in BA

For readers who are well-schooled behavior analysts, a distinction must be made between functional assessment as employed in BA and formal functional analyses. A formal functional analysis, as employed in institutional, school, and other controlled settings, involves the systematic manipulation of consequences while recording the frequency of the behavior of interest in a specific context to determine with confidence the function of the behavior in that context (Iwata, Kahng, Wallace, & Lindberg, 2000). Such formal functional analyses are not possible in adult, outpatient settings, as the behavior of interest often happens in the client's daily life and the potential controlling variables are not under the control of the clinician. BA may be employed in inpatient settings, however, where staff may be trained to conduct such formal analyses.

When in outpatient settings, it is still important to formulate hypotheses about behavioral functions as precisely as possible. The clinician works with the material available to him or her, including client self-reports and observations of in-session behavior. In addition, partners or family members may be brought in to session for additional information. The clinician attempts to analyze, as specifically as possible, the antecedents and consequences related to client clinically relevant behavior through detailed questioning of the client and others about specific instances of the behavior, keeping in mind the limitations of client self-report and revising hypotheses about behavioral functions over time. The clinician continually seeks to look beyond the form of the client's verbal descriptions of behavior to identify the operating functional relations involved.

In defense of this broader definition of functional analysis, Skinner (1953) noted, "any process that yields the external variables of which behavior is a function, is a functional analysis" (p. 35). In addition to BA, several other behavioral psychotherapy approaches make use of such indirect functional analyses, including Dialectical Behavior Therapy (DBT), Functional Analytic Psychotherapy (FAP; Kohlenberg & Tsai, 1991), and the Cognitive-Behavioral Analysis System of Psychotherapy (McCullough, 2000).

As will be discussed in Part 2 of this book, the current version of BA we describe provides such an indirect functional analysis strategy to determine when to focus on antecedents, behavior, consequences, or multiple variables. This assessment is followed by specific targeted intervention strategies. Antecedents are amplified through stimulus control interventions. The behavior is generally targeted through activation assignments and skills training. Finally, consequences are manipulated through contingency management procedures, such as contracting, and through mindfulness interventions and the identification of values, that help individuals activate in the face of consequences that otherwise would shut down behavior.

6

The ubiquity of positive reinforcement

To the average person, a positive reinforcer is a reward—a pat on the back, a "good job," a piece of candy, a Christmas bonus. When behaviorists make the claim that consequences play a large role in determining behavior, the average person may reply, "Sure, such rewards are sometimes important in determining behavior, but not *most* of the time. After all, most of the things I do are not rewarded at all." When the concept of reinforcement is synonymous with reward, it is hard to see how reinforcement is as important to human behavior as behaviorists say it is. Here, we introduce a definition of reinforcement that is much broader than reinforcement as reward (in this Point we focus on positive reinforcement; negative reinforcement and punishment are discussed in subsequent Points).

A reinforcer *is any consequence that, when it follows a specific behavior, makes that behavior more likely to occur in the future.* The most important aspect of this definition is that anything can function as a reinforcer if it leads to an increase in the rate of behavior (i.e., reinforcement is defined functionally)—all that is needed is a change that follows (is contingent on) the behavior it functions to reinforce. This change may be the receipt of praise or candy, but many other, less obvious changes are relevant. Let us consider two basic examples—walking and breathing.

Is walking maintained by reinforcement? If reinforcement is seen only in terms of rewards such as "good job" or provision of candy, it is hard to see how reinforcement applies. Our parents may have offered such rewards when, at age one or so, we took our fist tentative steps, but probably not reliably so.

Very soon afterwards even those rewards ceased to occur. If reinforcement is defined more broadly, however, it becomes obvious how fundamental reinforcement is to walking, and how walking would stop if it did not produce this reinforcement. Consider the sorts of immediate and reliable environmental changes that are produced by walking. Each step results in a slightly new environment, a new perspective, and—most importantly—this new environment is located one step closer to whatever it is you are walking towards. Simply put, the reinforcer for walking from point A to point B is the arrival at point B. The reinforcer for each step from point A to point B is being one step closer to point B.

Consider for how long you would continue "walking" if it did not get you anywhere. How long would it take you to stop, look down at your feet, and ask yourself the equivalent of, "What is going wrong here? Why is this movement suddenly no longer producing the reinforcer it has so reliably produced for so long?"

Breathing is similar. On the one hand, breathing is clearly an automatic, physiological process. That is not contested. To a behaviorist, however, it is also strongly controlled by reinforcement. As with all reinforcers, the question is, what changes are produced by breathing, and would breathing stop if it ceased to produce those changes? Breathing, of course, functions to deliver needed oxygen to the lungs. So it can be said that oxygen is the reinforcer that maintains breathing. The relationship between the behavior of breathing and the consequence of oxygen is usually perfect; each breath we take reliably produces fresh oxygen in our bodies. Any doubts about this can be erased by considering how quickly we stop breathing when it does not produce this consequence. For example, when breathing results in the intake of water, smoke, or some other substance, we immediately hold our breath and try to find fresh oxygen.

With both walking and breathing, we do not remember the process by which reinforcement shaped the behavior. In the case of walking, the shaping process occurred over time, while with breathing, the behavior occurred immediately and immediately produced reinforcement. In both cases, even though the shaping processes were different and we do not remember either of them, the essential role of reinforcement is clear when we consider what would happen to the behavior if reinforcement ceased to occur.

The timing of reinforcement

A fundamental aspect of reinforcement is that the closer in time and space a reinforcer is to the behavior it is intended to reinforce, the more effective that reinforcer will be. Walking and breathing are prime examples. These are unusually high strength and reliable behaviors, and this strength and reliability is clearly a function of the immediacy of reinforcement. The power of immediate reinforcement is familiar to anyone who has tried to house-train a puppy. You need to be alert for the exact moment when the puppy has successfully or unsuccessfully used the newspaper. Leaving the puppy alone for the evening, coming back to a soiled carpet, and then scolding the puppy hours after the problematic behavior will result in a confused puppy rather than a trained puppy.

This issue is extremely important clinically, as it is often the case that a client's behavior is controlled by undesirable (in terms of values and life goals) but reinforcing short-term consequences rather than desired long-term consequences. Drug abuse is the clearest example. A heroin addict or cigarette smoker knows that the drug use is shortening his or her lifespan (long-term consequences) but the immediate, short-term positive and negatively reinforcing qualities of drug use are simply too strong. The immediate rush of intravenous heroin use and the immediate calm of nicotine intake dominate over other competing contingencies. In BA, specific interventions are designed to increase the salience and power of long-term consequences and to decrease the power that short-term consequences often have on behavioral choices.

Schedules of reinforcement

Another important concept, *schedules of reinforcement*, can also be illustrated by walking and breathing. Most of the time, the reinforcers that consequate walking and breathing occur on a *fixed ratio* schedule of reinforcement, in which the reinforcer is provided after a fixed (pre-determined) number of behaviors has occurred. Most clinically interesting behavior, however, is not maintained by fixed ratio schedules; indeed, naturally occurring examples of fixed ratio schedules are hard to find. Instead, fixed ratio schedules are often arranged specifically by humans. For example, an inpatient gets a token for five successful interpersonal interactions or a salesperson gets a bonus after every 50 sales.

Most clinically interesting behavior is maintained by *variable ratio* schedules. Variable ratio schedules are said to occur when reinforcers do not reliably occur after a fixed number of responses but instead the number of responses required is free to vary—sometimes a given number of behaviors produces the reinforcer and sometimes it does not. In these instances, it is useful to consider the average number of responses that must occur before a reinforcer is produced, and this average number may be reported to describe how much work it requires, on average, to produce a reinforcer under the specific conditions. For example, a variable ratio-10 schedule indicates that over time the individual is required to engage in twice as much work to produce the same number of reinforcers as the individual would under a variable ratio-5 schedule. An example of this would be that a very socially skilled man, on average, may approach 5 women in a bar before obtaining a phone number, while a less socially skilled man, on average, may need to approach 10 women in a bar before obtaining a phone number. For both individuals, the reinforcement schedule is variable—it may not be required for these two individuals to approach exactly 5 or exactly 10 women for each to produce a phone number, but over the long term these ratios would hold.

For our purposes, an important implication of variable ratio schedules is that the occurrence of a behavior does not have to be reinforced continuously for the behavior to continue to reliably occur. What matters is not reinforcement per se, but the schedule of reinforcement—the pattern of reinforcement that has occurred with respect to the behavior in the past. In other words, we do not engage in behavior *in order to* obtain a specific reinforcer in the future. Instead, we engage in behavior because it has led to a pattern of specific reinforcers *in the past*.

The strength of reinforcement

A final important issue is that the stronger the reinforcer, the less often it needs to occur to maintain a behavior. Imagine walking down a specific street, looking down, and noticing a dime. This dime represents, in today's world, a very small reinforcer. The next time you walk down that specific street, it is likely you will have forgotten about the dime and you will not look down at the same spot. Now imagine walking down that street, looking down, and noticing a $1,000 bill, which represents a very large reinforcer. The next time you walk down that specific street, you certainly will be looking down. How many times will you walk down that street and look down, even if you never find another $1,000 bill? Probably quite a few.

The ubiquity of reinforcement

Although we are not necessarily aware of positive reinforcement in our lives, it is fundamental. Reinforcement can take on a variety of forms. Classic rewards, such as tokens, praise, and candy, may function as reinforcement. Basic behavioral processes, however, are reinforced by basic and naturally occurring reinforcers, such as food, oxygen, sunlight, and tactile and sexual stimulation. All sorts of operations on the environment are reinforced by the success of the operation; turning a door handle opens a door, turning a key starts an engine, and answering a phone produces a voice on the other end.

Social reinforcement is particularly important for our purposes. Put simply, we are constantly reinforcing and shaping each other socially, in both subtle and not so subtle ways. Subtle socially reinforcing responses can include maintaining closer physical distance (leaning forward or stepping closer to indicate attention), asking more questions, engaging in more eye contact, having an open posture, smiling more, and nodding more. In BA, clients are activated to contact social reinforcement and may be taught social skills to maximize receipt of social reinforcement.

7

The meaning of life

What is the meaning of life? BA presents a distinct view, because, as we have already discussed, to a behaviorist, *meaning* is to be found in the context of behavior, specifically the consequences of behavior. Thus, according to BA, a meaningful life is a life filled with contact with diverse and stable sources of positive reinforcement. In turn, a depressed life is a life with limited contact with diverse and stable sources of positive reinforcement—a life without meaning. The terms *diverse* and *stable* are important and will be elaborated.

Diversity refers to *not putting all of one's eggs into one basket*. Thus, if a reinforcer is lost, other reinforcers are still in place to function as protective factors against depression. Let us consider two primary risk factors for depression: Widowhood and retirement. When Joan became a widow, it was extremely important that social support in the form of friends, siblings, children, and grandchildren was available to Joan. Such support did not produce a full escape from the feelings that came with widowhood for Joan, but the support allowed her grieving process to occur in the context of alternate social reinforcers without a spiral into complicated bereavement or depression. Likewise, when Patrick retired from a long success-ful career, it was extremely important that alternate reinforcing activities were available to him. Patrick became an avid bird watcher, spent much more time with his children and grand-children, and began volunteering for the local nature con-servatory. Patrick never again felt the same sense of fulfillment as he did during the peaks of his career, but a spiral into depression was prevented because he found meaningful, reinforcing replacements. He was content.

Stability highlights that not all positive reinforcers are created equally. Consider heroin, an extremely potent positive reinforcer. If our definition of the meaning of life is contact with positive reinforcement, why not heroin? One problem with heroin is that its reinforcing properties are not stable. The reinforcing effects do not last and are followed by withdrawal effects, and larger and larger doses are needed to achieve the same reinforcing effects over time. A dose that provided an extremely positively reinforcing high on the first use will provide considerably less positive reinforcement 50 uses later (the 50th use also will result in potent negative reinforcement by relieving withdrawal symptoms). This, of course, is the definition of tolerance.

Issues of stability are not restricted to chemical reinforcers. In fact, many previously reinforcing stimuli become less reinforcing over time through processes such as satiation and habituation. For example, a partner's jokes, experienced as funny at the beginning of a relationship, begin to sound boorish after being repeated time after time. Likewise, sexual attractiveness fades with familiarity and a couple's sex life may become boring and routine over time. In these situations, although once reinforcing events are still present in the current environment, the reinforcing properties of the events have changed and the reinforcer is effectively lost or weakened (Kanter, Cautilli, Busch, & Baruch, 2005).

The importance of stability also clarifies that one-time positive reinforcers are not particularly useful to BA. For example, a client may be depressed because she has moved away from her family and does not have many friends in the new city. One activation assignment to consider would be a trip to visit family in her hometown. While there is nothing wrong with such a trip, it leads potentially to a *single episode* of a reinforcing event, rather than a *stable source* of reinforcing events. A more effective activation assignment would be to create new friends in the new city, or to schedule repeated and regular family visits.

A strong devotion to a single pursuit is not necessarily to be discouraged here. An artist may devote his or her life to art, at the expense of a myriad of other reinforcing possibilities. The problematic issue is not the devotion to a single pursuit but to the diversity and stability of reinforcers available within that pursuit. We would discourage a strong devotion to an artistic endeavor if the behavior is controlled solely by a need for adulation, or another isolated and unstable reinforcer. However, the artist may be stimulated and reinforced by the entire artistic process—the initial conception of an idea, the process of turning the idea into an artistic reality, the use of various artistic mediums, the excitement of publicly displaying the art, and communication with and learning from other artists.

In general, the goal of BA is the development of routines that allow for consistent contact with diverse, stable sources of positive reinforcement, not isolated reinforcing events. The trick, then, is to locate and contact diverse and stable reinforcing features of the environment. For example, a relationship in which one member of the couple was primarily attracted to the other because the other was funny and sexually attractive represents neither diversity nor stability. This relationship indeed is unlikely to survive the long term unless more diverse and more stable reinforcing properties take control, such as trustworthiness, intimate connection, mutual understanding, shared values, and the accumulation of shared experiences and memories.

The problem of pleasure

According to BA, the reason why contact with diverse, stable sources of positive reinforcement is important is not that it results in diverse, stable experiences of pleasure, but that it results in diverse, stable repertoires of psychologically healthy, personally meaningful (i.e., in line with an individual's morals and values) behavior. In other words, the meaning of life, according to BA, is not a hedonistic search for pleasure. Reinforcement is important in that it increases the frequency of behavior; thus, the issue is—what behavioral repertoires do we want to become more frequent?

This distinction between reinforcement and pleasure was noted early in the history of BA. For example, activity scheduling as described in CT involves the client rating both *mastery* and *pleasure* of specific activities engaged in. Mastery refers to a sense of accomplishment when performing a task, while pleasure refers to pleasant feelings associated with the activity (Beck et al., 1979). Both are important to activity scheduling and they may be totally independent, in that an activity that brings mastery may not be pleasant (e.g., fixing the sink) and an activity that brings pleasure may not be experienced as an accomplishment (e.g., getting a massage).

The role of values

Although not traditionally viewed through a behavioral lens, values were introduced to modern behavioral theory through the writings of Steve Hayes and his colleagues on Acceptance and Commitment Therapy (ACT; Hayes, Strosahl, & Wilson, 1999). These authors emphasized the verbal behavior of stating one's values and defined such statements about what one values as "verbally construed global desired life consequences" (p. 206). Behavior may become automatically reinforcing simply through linking it with long-term valued consequences, and this may sustain behavior in the face of very strong competing short-term contingencies. Thus, individuals who value competing in marathons may continue to run in the presence of a multitude of aversive stimuli that would extinguish running in others. In a way, to BA, life is like a marathon.

Values are an important consideration in determining which behavioral repertoires will result in stable reinforcement and thus are incorporated in BA. By verbally stating values, the relationship between behavior and very distal or long-term consequences becomes more salient, thus effectively allowing such long-term consequences to influence behavior in the face of competing immediate consequences. For example, stating, "I value being a good father" is a description that behaviors related to being a good father, such as spending time with one's kids, will be experienced as positively reinforcing in the long run, even if the immediate experience is not reinforcing (e.g., the kids are not showing appreciation to the father for his efforts).

One's values are a complex product of one's history. The trick is identifying what one values and arranging the environment to generate behavior consistent with those values. The contingencies should do the rest in creating a rich, meaningful life. Thus, while the heart of BA is direct activation—simple assignments that bring the client into contact with diverse, stable sources of positive reinforcement—the key is in developing activation assignments that are functional, informed by life values and goals related to those values, and not primarily directed by experiencing pleasure (in fact many activation assignments are quite unpleasant). BA does not simply schedule as many pleasurable activities as possible, but rather asks the client a series of simple questions: What do you want out of life? How have you given up on these goals? What have you stopped doing or been avoiding doing because you became scared or hopeless? How can you activate yourself and create meaning and purpose in your life?

8

Depression and positive reinforcement

If the meaning of life is to be found in contact with diverse, stable sources of positive reinforcement, then life loses its meaning when such contact is lost. In BA, depression is seen as a result of environments that do not produce contact with diverse, stable sources of positive reinforcement, and there are many pathways to this end. In this Point, we discuss the primary process of direct removal of positive reinforcement. To the extent that depression is to be interpreted literally, as in behavior being "pressed down" or reduced, it is relatively easy to see how this is clinically relevant.

Removal of positive reinforcement

As we suggested in Point 6, sometimes the easiest way to determine what is reinforcing a behavior is to remove the hypothesized reinforcer and see what happens. When a reinforcer for a certain behavior is removed, the rate of the behavior slows and eventually stops. Technically, this is known as *extinction*. This simple fact that behavior slows when reinforcement is removed is one of the most established in behavior analysis. It is true for fruit flies, rats, pigeons, monkeys, elephants, dolphins, and humans.

For example, one may stop going out to social events if one's friends have moved away. The social event still exists, but some of the primary reinforcing aspects of it do not. One stops putting clothing in the washing machine if the washing machine breaks and stops washing the clothes, and one stops turning the key on the car ignition if the car is not starting. These are obvious examples but that, in essence, is the point. We often take positive reinforcers for granted and only notice their effect on our behavior when they are removed, resulting in extinction of the behavior upon which the reinforcers were contingent.

The rate at which a behavior is extinguished is in part determined by the schedule of reinforcement that maintained the behavior. Behaviors maintained on very rich schedules of reinforcement (e.g., walking and breathing) will extinguish almost immediately after the reinforcement is removed. This makes sense because the reinforcer has so reliably followed the behavior in the past, so the contrast between contexts will be very clear. Behavior that is maintained by leaner rates of reinforcement (e.g., 1 reinforcer for every 100 behaviors) is much, much harder to extinguish, as it will take many, many behaviors before the lack of reinforcement becomes salient and exerts an effect.

This is especially true when the reinforcers are both rare (i.e., a lean schedule) and unpredictable (i.e., a variable schedule). Bird watchers spend hours and hours looking through binoculars, reinforced by finally sighting the rare and unpredictable bird. Gamblers throw millions of dollars into slot machines, reinforced by the rare and unpredictable payoff. A woman stays in a relationship with an abusive man, reinforced by the rare and unpredictable expression of love and affection.

How removal of positive reinforcement feels

When positive reinforcers are lost, something else important happens in addition to the extinction of behavior. Put simply, when positive reinforcers are lost, people *feel* bad.

It is not the case that contact with positive reinforcement always results in positive emotional reactions, but removal of previously stable sources of positive reinforcement almost always results in negative emotional reactions. For example, turning the door handle and opening the door (contact with positive reinforcement) does not feel good, but turning that same door handle and finding that the door no longer opens likely will result in a negative emotional reaction, such as confusion or frustration. Likewise, breathing in air does not feel good but breathing and receiving another substance instead will result in panic and alarm.

These feelings may be seen as respondent reactions, and it is important to note that operant and respondent behaviors interact and are often evoked by the same environmental antecedents. Specifically relevant to depression is that when the environment produces reductions in or losses of positive reinforcement, the operant response is reduction in or low levels of behavior, and the respondent response is that one feels bad.

We use the generic phrase "one feels bad" strategically. The actual response may be labeled more specifically as sad, frustrated, angry, hopeless, blue, down, depressed, and so on. How and what we label this response depends on individual learning histories as well as cultural norms, so there should be some variety in the labels used. Underneath the label, however, is an experience that is labeled. Sadness may be the label most closely tied to the experience of depression.

It is clearly established that some presentations of clinical depression are a function of losses, such as a divorce, loss of job, or move to a new city (Kessler, 1997), which can easily be construed as losses of positive reinforcement (cf., Horwitz, Wakefield, & Spitzer, 2007). The current theory, that losses of positive reinforcement produce operant reductions in behavior and respondent emotional reactions, may be sufficient to explain these cases of depression. Consider the symptoms of a major depressive episode, which include depressed mood, loss of interest or pleasure in things, loss of appetite, loss of sleep, slowed behavior, fatigue and loss of energy, loss of self-esteem, and loss of concentration/attention. This symptom list represents a global reduction in several important classes of behavior, including cognitive behaviors (e.g., loss of appetite, behaviorally, is reduced eating behavior, and loss of self-esteem represents a reduction in positive self-evaluations).

We are certainly not saying that this particular symptom profile will always result from all losses, and it is the case that some symptoms of depression are not best characterized as reductions in behavior (e.g., some individuals demonstrate over-eating rather than under-eating). We are saying that the behavioral model appears to offer a simple, parsimonious account for some depressive reactions, especially if the losses are large enough, the primary behavioral features of the depression are global reductions in behavior, and the primary respondent features of the depression are sadness or distress in general.

An important point is that these reactions are normal, adaptive and utterly human. In fact, these reactions are most certainly built into our systems through evolution, and they serve adaptive functions, such as eliciting support from others, enabling problem solving, and signaling defeat to avoid additional unnecessary conflict and loss (Kanter, Busch, Weeks, & Landes, 2008).

Three factors that influence positive reinforcement

Direct loss of positive reinforcement is not the only pathway to depression, but it is one viable pathway, and its simple elegance as an explanation led it to become the foundation of the traditional behavioral model of depression advanced by Lewinsohn (1974), which emphasized three factors that produce contact with positive reinforcement.

First, what is potentially reinforcing to the person? A quiet walk in the woods with a friend may be reinforcing to one person, but a night out on the town with friends may be reinforcing to another. This factor allows the behavioral model to be quite inclusive and integrative, in that there are all sorts of non-behavioral influences on what is potentially reinforcing to an individual. Biological differences in reward sensitivity, cognitive styles, and other determinants of individual differences will influence what, and how much of what, is reinforcing to a particular individual. These may represent vulnerabilities to depression in a diathesis-stress model that is in fact consistent with the behavioral model.

Second, is that reinforcement available in the environment? If going for a quiet walk in the woods is potentially reinforcing, does the person live in the country where such walks can happen regularly, or does that person live in the middle of a busy city? As will be discussed throughout this book, this issue is really the heart of basic BA. Clinicians employ simple activation assignments, such as going for a walk in the woods or going to a party, to put the client in contact with potentially available sources of positive reinforcement. A host of strategies and considerations for how to successfully activate clients, taking into consideration issues of shaping and graded improvements, were developed over the years and are employed in BA.

Third, does the person have the skills necessary to obtain available reinforcement? If parties are potentially reinforcing to a person, and the person has been invited to one, there is a chance the person will go to the party and not have the social skills necessary to have a good time. Does the person have the social skills necessary to obtain and maintain friendships, to ask someone on a date, to maintain a long-term intimate relationship, or to assertively ask his or her boss for a raise? To address possible deficits in these skills, assertiveness and social skills training procedures were folded into the arsenal of BA techniques.

9

The ubiquity of negative reinforcement

So far, we have discussed how depressive environments result in reductions in behavior. Depressive environments, however, also result in increases in behavior, specifically increases in avoidance behavior. This observation was made by Ferster (1973) and became central to the conceptualization of BA presented by Martell and colleagues (2001).

Often times it is difficult to determine if a behavioral change is best described as a reduction in positively reinforced behavior or an increase in avoidance behavior. Consider Vicky who has stayed in bed all day. On the one hand, this appears to be a simple decrease in behavior, as the myriad of behaviors that Vicky used to do, such as eating breakfast, showering, brushing her teeth, putting on clothing, making her family breakfast, cleaning the house, running errands, and so on, have all stopped. On the other hand, one very important behavior has increased—that of staying in bed! As always, we look to the function of the behavior to fully understand it and to help us to determine the best way to describe it. What are the antecedents and consequences to staying in bed? In this case, Vicky has recently been divorced and her children have gone off to college. She is now alone. Thus, the antecedents that prompted much of her prior behavior, and consequences that reinforced it, have been lost, and this appears to be a case in which the traditional behavioral model applies: Reinforcers have been lost, behavior has been extinguished, and Vicky feels depressed.

Upon further inspection, however, other processes are at work. Specifically, now that Vicky feels depressed, her feelings of depression, tiredness, and fatigue become additional antecedents in the behavioral ABC analysis. Getting out of bed, taking a shower, and brushing her teeth *are now harder to do*. Thus, not only have Vicky's prior positive behaviors been extinguished in this situation, but staying in bed has been reinforced. Specifically, staying in bed successfully avoids the additional exertion and fatigue that result from getting out of bed. Staying in bed is warm and comfortable, while the outside world has become cold and harsh. Furthermore, if Vicky gets out of bed and goes to the supermarket, her friends may see her and she may have to talk about the divorce—a further competing contingency that increases the likelihood of staying in bed. In this situation, functionally, staying in bed is experiential avoidance behavior, and the consequence is negative reinforcement—immediate successful avoidance of potentially and actual aversive situations and feelings.

Negative reinforcement in our lives

Negative reinforcement is equally as ubiquitous as positive reinforcement. Given a headache (A), we take aspirin (B) to relieve the headache (C). Given a stressful social event (A), we drink alcohol (B) to ease the social anxiety (C). Given a ringing telephone (A), we pick it up (B) to stop the ringing (C). Given sadness and loss (A), we stay in bed (B) to avoid the effort and pain of the day (C).

For all too many of us, day-to-day life is replete with negative reinforcement and lacking positive reinforcement. Lara, a wife and mother of three children, wakes up before the family to prepare breakfast and lunch, then races from errand to errand, fills the car with gas, pays the bills, returns home to make dinner, then walks on eggshells all evening to avoid conflict with her husband, who is under stress at work. Her life is filled with the stress of daily hassles and meeting the demands of her family, all generally in the service of limiting her worries about family functioning and not being a good mother and wife. She does not feel the accomplishment that comes with mastering positively reinforcing outcomes or the enjoyment that comes with simple pleasant events. She feels the exhaustion, stress and depression that come with chronic avoidance and escape from negative outcomes.

It may be helpful to note that both Vicky's and Lara's avoidance repertoires are largely about avoiding aversive emotional or bodily states, although one is very passive and one is very active. The important point is that when avoidance becomes extensive and generalized, it is a certain pathway to additional losses of positive reinforcement. When a person's behavioral repertoire is dominated by avoidance, it is difficult to actually engage in behavior that leads to positive reinforcement. Staying in bed makes it impossible for Vicky to lead a meaningful and productive life. Likewise, Lara may keep her family functioning on a day-to-day basis, but there is no room for Lara to develop alternate, positively reinforcing pursuits that would add meaning to her life.

Thus, excessive efforts to avoid negative experiences and outcomes, despite the obvious inclination to do so, may ensure the construction of environments that support depression. Avoidance efforts continue over time because they are successful, in the short-term. Vicky avoids feeling the exhaustion of getting out of bed and Lara's family does not fall apart. But both wake up the next morning, in the same situations, with no new skills or strategies for solving their problems and improving their lives. The avoidance repertoires have been strengthened by the negatively reinforcing consequences experienced the previous day, and their spirals into deeper and deeper depression continue.

The need for functional analysis

We originally questioned whether Vicky's staying in bed was an example of a decrease in behavior or an increase in behavior. The answer is that without a functional analysis, it is impossible to decide. To the extent that her depression is best characterized by simple losses of positive reinforcement, we may view her staying in bed as a decrease in behavior. If this is the case simple graded activity scheduling may suffice to activate Vicky to overcome her depression. To the extent, however, that Vicky is avoiding feeling negative emotions by staying in bed, it may be more useful to conceptualize her problem as an increase in avoidance behavior. Simple activity scheduling that is not sensitive to this avoidance may be less likely to succeed and strategies to address her avoidance specifically may be needed.

Notice how the analysis is linked to treatment techniques. There is no right or wrong answer to the question of how to conceptualize a client's behaviors; instead, there are more or less useful answers. Ultimately, BA conceptualizations incorporate ABC functional analyses because these analyses are linked to treatment techniques. In some cases, simple activation techniques to re-instate positive reinforcement are all that are needed. In others, avoidance plays a key role and needs to be targeted. In still others, multiple factors are involved and treatment will involve a mixture of techniques. This complexity lies at the heart of BA and Points 21 through 25 will provide details on when and how different BA techniques may be employed, based on functional analysis.

10

The role of punishment

So far we have provided examples for how environments characterized by losses of positive reinforcement can lead to depression, and how environments characterized by excessive negative reinforcement can lead to depression. These two processes may be primary pathways to depression, but they are not the only pathways. Here we consider the role of punishment. Like losses of positive reinforcement, punishment also reduces operant behavior and produces respondent behavior. Punishment results in a decrease in the behavior being punished, and receiving punishment also feels bad.

We all know how punishment feels and not much needs to be said. While single instances of punishment may produce aggression and anger, more relevant to depression are instances of prolonged and inescapable punishment. In such instances, punishment often works all too well, extinguishing behavior for long after the punishment has stopped. It is common for clients with chronic depression to report childhood histories of prolonged and inescapable punishment. Such clients invariably have problems with obtaining and maintaining intimate relationships, as the requisite intimate relationship building and maintaining behaviors cannot develop and be reinforced under such circumstances. The important point here is that, for the client, the punishment is no longer occurring and, in fact, has not occurred for a long period of time, but it still exerts an influence over behavior. The client not only may not have learned how to be intimate, but may have become chronically passive and may appear unwilling to try. The client may say, "Why bother trying? I know it is not going to work out well for me." The client may feel hopeless.

Research with humans shows that such responses should not be interpreted as just a lack of motivation or unwillingness (explanatory fictions); they are a function of histories of punishment. For example, experiments have shown that participants exposed to initially inescapable shock subsequently fail to try to escape even when the shock becomes escapable (Klein & Seligman, 1976), and participants presented unsolvable problems later fail to solve problems that were solvable (Roth & Kubal, 1975). Seligman labeled such behavior "learned helplessness" (Overmier & Seligman, 1967).

Research on punishment shows that it has an important effect beyond creating helplessness and reducing the behavior punished. Specifically, the punisher becomes an aversive stimulus, eliciting fear and evoking avoidance, and if the punishment is severe enough, this fear and avoidance will generalize. This is obvious—the child who has been physically abused by her father may grow up to fear and avoid men in general. In such a situation, we have a decrease in behavior controlled by a history of punishment, and an additional layer of avoidance controlled by negative reinforcement. As in many pathways to depression, the end result is lack of contact with positive reinforcement. Thus, the operant and respondent behavioral products of loss of positive reinforcement and punishment ultimately, in most cases, overlap and become indistinguishable.

In BA, therefore, there are multiple pathways to losses of positive reinforcement, and the goal of treatment is ultimately to increase contact with positive reinforcement, regardless of how the client became depressed. The specific nature of the interventions required to help the person achieve contact with positive reinforcement, however, will depend on a functional analysis of the depression. Working to activate a client with a history of chronic punishment will take patience and sensitivity. Simple activation assignments (e.g., to ask a man to have coffee to get to know him better) that target the lack of contact with positive reinforcement but do not functionally address the punishment or avoidance may fail.

11

An (almost) complete behavioral model of depression

Once the basics of functional contextualism and reinforcement are understood, the behavioral theory of depression is quite simple. In a nutshell, it is that people are responsive to their environments; both the historical and current environment exert an influence over current behavior. In fact such responsiveness is built into the human condition and is fundamental to being human.

By the mid-1970s, several of the pieces were in place for a complete behavioral model of depression, but the pieces remained to be integrated. The original behavioral theory of depression advanced by Lewinsohn (1974) emphasized how environments characterized by losses of positive reinforcements can lead to depression. Ferster's (1973) writings, highlighted in the behavioral model of depression advanced by Martell, Addis, and Jacobson (2001), emphasized how environments characterized by excessive negative reinforcement can lead to depression. Seligman's early writings on learned helplessness (Overmier & Seligman, 1967) emphasized how environments characterized by inescapable punishment can lead to depression. These three processes—loss of positive reinforcement, excessive negative reinforcement, and excessive punishment—are crucial to a behavioral understanding of depression but a complete understanding of depression requires more than understanding these three processes.

Reinforcement for depressive behavior

A fourth process is that some depressive behaviors are maintained by reinforcement provided by others. This is a well known concept and non-behaviorists may see it as an issue of *secondary gains*. Often, a depressed person's spouse, parent, or other family member may unwittingly provide a mixture of positive reinforcement for depressed behavior, in the form of sympathy, caring and concern, and negative reinforcement for depressed behavior, in the form of taking over responsibilities for and reducing burdens placed upon the depressed person.

Such responses from others are likely when depression first starts. For example, Frank recently lost his job, and both he and his wife were very upset. Trying to be sensitive to him and make him feel better, his wife suggested he take a few days to relax and recover. Frank's wife viewed this as giving Frank "a break" during a difficult time. Reinforcement for depressed behavior now began. The problem was that after a few days of this, depressed, passive behavior was strengthened in Frank, and became more likely to occur. His wife began to think that her continued extra efforts to take care of things were in fact "enabling" Frank and that he was taking her for granted. She did not, however, want to appear insensitive or be harsh to him, so she continued to reinforce his depressed behavior, simultaneously becoming increasingly bitter about the situation. Whereas initially Frank was feeling mildly depressed and in a good marriage, now he found himself feeling increasingly depressed and his marriage was starting to unravel.

It is important to note that, while Frank's wife may have felt resentful and that he was taking advantage of her, from our perspective the situation was not Frank's fault and he was not doing it on purpose. His behavior was simply a product of the current contingencies. Frank, in fact, may come to feel increasingly guilty about his wife's extra efforts and his own inability to get moving again. His guilt and personal explanations about the situation (e.g., a lack of willpower or a personal weakness) are a product of the contingencies at work but are not in functional control over his behavior. The guilt and personal explanations, however, ultimately may contribute to his depression, as he may start to avoid his wife in order to avoid acute experiences of the guilt, and he may start to avoid talking to his wife about his feelings, in order to avoid the shame that is elicited by his personal explanations for his condition.

Frank's example demonstrates how multiple behavioral factors may combine to produce depression. First, the situation started with a classic loss of positive reinforcement (the job), resulting in immediate behavioral reductions and negative feelings. In Frank's case, however, the spiral into depression was more a product of how he and his wife responded to this situation than to the original situation. Although both of them were acting in a way that made sense given the situation, they inadvertently established processes of positive reinforcement of depressive behavior (the increased care and concern from the wife) and negative reinforcement of depressive behavior (the escape from work and responsibility, the avoidance of guilt related to Frank's wife, and the avoidance of shame related to Frank's personal explanations about his depression). These processes ultimately resulted in an environment that became less and less positively reinforcing over time, fostering a cycle into clinical depression.

A complex interplay of processes

To summarize the behavioral model of depression, we may focus on three themes: operant reductions in behavior, operant increases in behavior, and respondent emotional reactions.

First, at the operant level, excessive punishment and loss of positive reinforcement will result in positive, non-depressed behavior slowing down. To the extent that the punishers, reinforcers lost or reinforcers reduced are large and generalized, the behavioral reductions should be large and generalized as well. Passivity, staying in bed, sleeping too much, not wanting to go out, anhedonia, eating less, slowed motor reactions, and slowed thinking can all result. Fatigue and loss of energy follow. Of course, the specific pattern of behavioral reductions will depend on the nature of the individual and the nature of the changes that have occurred, and should be assessed on a case by case basis.

Second, also at the operant level, excessive positive and negative reinforcement of depressive behavior result in negative, depressed behavior increasing. When life is filled with stress and hassle, behavioral repertoires become dominated by attempts to avoid or reduce such stress and hassle. When one feels bad, repertoires may become focused on *not feeling worse*, and important others in the environment may arrange contingencies that support this. The end result, however, is further reductions in positive reinforcement, and further reductions in behaviors that would proactively address the true environmental sources of depression.

Finally, when these environmental contingencies are at work, one feels bad. Again, the specific nature of the feeling will vary, depending on the nature of the contingencies, and how the individual has learned to identify, label, and express emotions. The bottom line is that life, unfortunately, is often hard, and our bodies are sensitive to the world around us. When major losses occur, we slow down and feel bad. When contact with positive reinforcement is reduced but not lost completely, we slow down and feel bad (but perhaps not as bad). When extremely or inescapably punished, we slow down and feel bad. When chronically deprived of contact with major sources of positive reinforcement, we become chronically slowed and feel chronically bad. Such is the human condition.

Thus, different cases of depression will be characterized by different histories, all functionally with the end result of losses of positive reinforcement. Some cases may be the result of major losses. Many cases of depression, however, appear to be a function of the accrual of multiple, chronic, mild stressors, including work-related stress, financial troubles, poor interpersonal interactions, and daily hassles such as homemaking demands, rather than major losses, per se. Some cases of depression are characterized by punishment, all-too-often in extreme and inescapable forms. Also of importance are situations in which a person has been chronically deprived of contact with major sources of positive reinforcement (e.g., an abusive or neglectful environment). Most cases of depression, of course, involve combinations of these factors. Functionally speaking, however, lives characterized by these events are characterized by low levels of positive reinforcement. Less functionally speaking, lives characterized by these events become meaningless.

Depression makes sense

The behavioral model holds that depression is an understandable response to negative life events, stressors, and difficult environments. This model leads to intense therapeutic empathy, because to the BA clinician, depression always makes sense, given the client's history, current environment and preexisting biology. The particular pattern of depressive symptoms with which a person presents will depend on his or her history. Thus, given that every depressed person has a unique history, there are as many different types of depression as there are depressed individuals. For example, one depressed client may present with a history of chronic childhood abuse, while another may have had a perfectly happy childhood but a recent series of losses, such as the death of her husband and children moving off to college. Both clients are currently depressed, both may be treated with BA and the behavioral model, but the symptoms targeted will be different for these clients.

For most depressed clients, the histories that led to depression are quite complex. It is not as if one bad thing happened. Sometimes there are clearly identifiable major life events— death of a loved one, divorce, loss of a job, an injury or health crisis, or a move to a new city. Other times, the loss of reinforcers can happen slowly, imperceptibly. Your friends, one by one, get married and have kids. You gradually spend more and more time at work and less time with your family. Your once adoring kids become adolescents and you cannot do a thing right, and all they want is to get away from you. Your financial problems and debts slowly begin to accumulate—at first you could afford the minimum payments on your credit card but it has grown out of control.

Other times, it may seem as if your life is full of reinforcers, but it really is not. You have a well-paying job and are respected professionally. Your wife is devoted and your kids are doing well. But your life feels empty. Here we need to look closely at your values—you may have spent a great deal of time building a career that ultimately means nothing to you. It may be hard to admit that your relationship with your wife, while it looks great on the surface, has lost its luster and both of you are "going through the motions."

Some claim that sometimes depression does not have environmental precipitants, that instead it comes out of the blue. It is our experience, however, that depression always makes sense in the context of the depressed person's life. It may be impossible to accurately or fully describe the causes, as history is indeed in the past and not available for a full analysis, but from BA's perspective, depression always makes sense in terms of one's history.

12

The role of cognition

The previous Point's title included the word *almost* to draw attention to one factor that has yet to be discussed in detail: cognition. Traditionally, behavioral models have been criticized for ignoring cognition. This criticism simply was unfair—they did not ignore cognition.

Thinking is behavior

As discussed in Point 2, behavioral theory treats thinking as behavior. In that sense cognition is important although it has no special status as something that causes behavior. The traditional behavioral model allowed that sometimes one behavior (i.e., thinking) may play a role in evoking and eliciting other behaviors (i.e., overt actions and emotional responses); such a contention is consistent with behavioral theory as long as the analysis does not stop there. In other words, we would not be satisfied that a thought caused a behavior until we understood the chain of historical and current events that caused the thought, and the chain of historical and current events that caused the thought to acquire functional control over behavior (Hayes & Brownstein, 1986).

That simple point aside, however, it was not until recently that a full behavioral model of language and cognition was developed that described how thinking acquires functional control over behavior. This model, called *Relational Frame Theory* (RFT; Hayes, Barnes-Holmes, & Roche, 2001), has been elaborated in many ways and applied to a variety of clinical problems (Woods & Kanter, 2007). This model also serves as the basis of ACT, which in fact is similar to BA in several respects (Kanter, Baruch, & Gaynor, 2006). A discussion of RFT, however, is beyond the scope of this book and we refer interested readers to the above sources.

Thinking influences behavior

For our purposes, we believe that what the reader needs to understand about the behavioral model of cognition is that thinking indeed can have a profound influence on all of the processes that lead to depression discussed previously in this book. Thus, thinking can influence what is experienced as positively reinforcing, what is experienced as punishing, what is experienced as a loss of reinforcement, and so on. To the extent that thinking influences these processes, thinking influences behavior. For example, a woman may *believe* her husband is cheating on her but be mistaken. To the extent that this belief is stable and unwavering, we should expect the same pattern of behavior as if the husband was actually cheating. The husband is effectively lost as a positive reinforcer, and probably established as a punisher and negative reinforcer. Technically, we would say that thinking the husband is cheating results in transformations of the function of the husband that are consistent with the husband actually cheating.

As another example, consider Susan who has received a poor work evaluation (Kanter, Busch, Weeks, & Landes, 2008). This negative event may naturally evoke a slow down in behavior and elicit a negative mood. If these responses are transient, they can be considered normal and adaptive. However, Susan may begin to *think* about the event in such a way that the event takes on additional problematic functions. Susan may think that she will never do well in her career, that she is doomed to failure, and that no one appreciates her. The poor work evaluation, in the context of this thinking, functionally may be experienced as a very large loss of positive reinforcement and another punishment in a long line of chronic punishments.

Such a pattern of thinking is a complex product of Susan's history. It may result in a transient set-back such as a poor job evaluation becoming functionally overwhelming. The initial negative experience of the poor evaluation could have been normal and adaptive without verbal elaboration but Susan's verbal elaboration has magnified and extended the experience into what may be a clinical depression.

Rumination

Thus, cognitive processes, such as ruminating, worrying, and engaging in self-critical or suicidal thinking, are of interest to BA but the focus is on the consequences, or function of the process, rather than the content. (This is consistent with some recent approaches to cognitive therapy as well; Wells, 2004). This focuses the clinician on questions such as: When did Susan start thinking such thoughts? What was Susan doing while she was thinking such thoughts? What consequences did the thinking have? What else could Susan have done during that time? Focusing on these questions leads to an important set of observations. Specifically, it is often the case with depressed clients that once they start thinking about a negative event, they have difficulty stopping thinking about the event. Furthermore, this thinking may be quite unproductive. Finally, this thinking tends to distance the person from the current environment. The person essentially is lost in ruminative thought.

Functionally, rumination must be reinforcing or it would not continue to occur. It may be that being lost in thought is negatively reinforcing for the individual if the environment with which one would otherwise be in contact is aversive, punishing or otherwise depressing. It also may be that rumination may be a temporarily successful way to decrease the pain associated with past events. Or it may represent an attempt to stay connected with something that has been lost, when other behavioral options are no longer available. For example, a grieving widow may ruminate about her deceased spouse in the absence of knowing what else to do. Rumination also may be experienced by the ruminator as problem solving or trying to gain insight or understanding into what happened. One may have been taught such thinking processes are useful, thus rumination may be experienced as positively reinforcing and strengthen over time, even if the ruminator eventually gets stuck in rumination and it actually blocks effective problem solving and movement forward.

Why not cognitive restructuring?

A reader may ask, if thinking influences behavior according to the behavioral model, then why not use cognitive restructuring techniques to change behavior? Truth be told, the exclusion of cognitive restructuring techniques from BA was as much a product of the research design of the Jacobson component analysis (Jacobson et al., 1996) as it was theoretical considerations. BA in that study was defined by the exclusion of cognitive techniques because the purpose of the study was to isolate the behavioral and cognitive components of treatment and compare them to each other.

The theoretical considerations against restructuring, in fact, were somewhat hypocritical. On the one hand, as we discussed above, cognition should not be treated as an ultimate cause. On the other hand, the pragmatic nature of behavioral theory would allow for a cognitive intervention to be employed if that intervention produced the sought-after behavior change. In other words, it may be pragmatically useful to intervene at the level of cognition even if cognition is not viewed as an ultimate cause. Ideally, we would like behavior therapy to be defined by its goals, rather than the form of its techniques, and a therapy that excludes certain functionally useful techniques simply because they are labeled non-behavioral is a limited therapy.

Our argument against using cognitive restructuring in BA as an intervention that may lead to behavior change is that it is simply incompatible with other BA techniques. While each approach may be equally effective when evaluated independently, cognitive restructuring is simply inconsistent with the overall BA model presented to clients, which focuses on taking action to overcome depression, even in the presence of negative thoughts and feelings.

Ultimately, this is an empirical question. Research to date supports the view that changing thoughts is not required to change depression (Longmore & Worrell, 2007), but much more research in this area is required. We are not saying that negative thinking does not change over the course of successful treatment of depression, including BA. In fact, cognitive change may be just as likely to occur using BA interventions as cognitive interventions (Jacobson et al., 1996; Jacobson & Gortner, 2000; Simons, Garfield, & Murphy, 1984; Zeiss et al., 1979). While cognitive change is likely in BA, cognitive change is not a goal of BA. The goal is a meaningful life produced not by how one thinks about life but by contact with diverse, stable, meaningful positive reinforcers.

13

The role of insight

Many individuals believe that psychotherapy is a process through which one gains insight into one's self, one's past, and why one does what one does. Some may believe that only by understanding one's past will one be able to change behavior in the present.

BA presents a distinct view on the role of insight in therapy. The problem with insight into the past is that the past is not amenable to change. Our current and future environments, however, are potentially changeable. Thus, in BA, understanding one's past is helpful only to the extent that it helps the client change the present and the future. The goal of BA is empowering individuals to change their current and future environments. In BA, insight without action is useless.

As we discussed in Point 6, reinforcement is a historical process—we engage in specific behaviors, not because we seek reinforcement in the future, but because the specific behaviors have been reinforced in the past. Thus, the past is extremely important to modern behavioral theory. Thus, in BA it is important to understand the client's history and the factors that have shaped the client into who he or she is. These stories provide important clues about the functional relations that may be the focus of treatment. In addition, clients expect to tell their stories, and listening empathically is important in building a solid therapeutic relationship and in understanding the client.

As a BA clinician listens to the client's story, however, the BA clinician also is sensitive to the vagaries of memory, the inaccuracies of self-report, and the biases that become facts as memories evolve over time. The historical variables that actually are important to understand for functional analysis may be very different from the variables identified by the client. The client's talk, after all, is just behavior, controlled by the historical *and current* context. Thus, changes in the current context may result in very different versions of the client's life story.

Of course, all clinicians are sensitive to the nature of self-report and the BA clinician is not particularly unique in this regard. BA takes this suspicion about insight one step farther than do most other therapies, however. Specifically, insight as a therapeutic process, with the exceptions noted above, is not only useless but it actually may be problematic in terms of its function and consequences. As BA clinicians, we have heard numerous stories from clients about previous therapy experiences that lasted years and years, with the express purpose of "figuring out why I am the way I am." By the end of these experiences, clients have gained considerable insight and a "therapy" vocabulary for talking about themselves and their psychological experiences, but their interpersonal problems still remain. In fact, such therapy-savvy clients may have a more difficult time relating to their peers because they have come to see the world through the particular theoretical lens of psychoanalysis or another psychotherapeutic worldview—thus therapy potentially has helped reduce contact with important positive reinforcers!

Finally, in BA it is important to consider the function of talking about the past in therapy. Consider Elaine who began psychoanalysis, four days a week, after she started having an affair with another man. The therapy did not focus on how to stop the affair or the current problems in her marriage. Instead, it focused on her distant past and identifying intrapsychic conflicts. Elaine, however, believed strongly that she was actively trying to solve the problem of her marriage by going to therapy. In this case, therapy may have inadvertently functioned for Elaine as a form of rumination; a style of pseudo-problem solving that alleviated the guilt associated with doing nothing about her behavior, but ultimately doing nothing to help Elaine change her behavior. From a BA perspective, going to therapy itself was a form of avoidance for Elaine.

14

Activation and acceptance

Consider the following interaction at the beginning of a course of BA:

Clinician: The first thing we are going to do is help you get moving again, get you out of bed and living again.

Client: I am so depressed, I don't think I can do it. If I just felt better or I could stop myself from being so pessimistic, I would be able to get out of bed.

Clinician: I completely understand how you are feeling. I know it feels impossible to get moving right now, but this treatment will help you get moving, even though you may be feeling the way you feel. Once you get moving, you will start to feel better. The problem with the alternative— waiting until you feel better and then starting to move—is that we may be waiting quite a while, if you never get out of bed. And, while you are there, your problems will only get worse.

In BA, such an initial client reaction to the idea of activation is quite normal, and indeed can be expected. The client has come to believe that his or her private experiences, the fatigue, sadness, and pain, must change *in order to* become more active. This client reaction and clinician response highlight how BA presents a quite distinct stance on how—and when—the private experiences associated with depression should change over the course of therapy.

To understand this stance, here is a brief reminder of the modern behavioral theory of depression. We have described depression as including both operant and respondent behavioral reactions, controlled by the current and historical context. We discussed how complex operant behaviors have a voluntary feel, while respondent behaviors, such as emotional reactions, feel more automatic. Emotional reactions feel automatic because they are, in essence, automatically, reliably elicited by the environment, even if the individual is trying not to have the reaction or does not want the reaction. Thus, a person may start to sweat and blush during a public presentation despite how this negatively impacts others' evaluations of the presentation, and a patient in a doctor's office may faint during a blood draw despite trying to remain poised and calm. These respondent reactions are uncontrollable, automatic, and completely natural.

This is not to say that the frequency and strength of respondent reactions can not be modified over time. Exposure therapy, in fact, reduces the frequency and strength of conditioned emotional reactions quite well (Foa, Hembree, & Rothbaum, 2007), through habituation to repeated presentations of the eliciting stimuli (ensuring, of course, that these conditioned stimuli are no longer paired with unconditioned aversive stimuli). Rather, we are saying that it is very difficult to control a specific respondent reaction in a specific situation without first creating a new relevant history. Until that new learning has occurred, in any particular moment the reaction may or may not occur and this is uncontrollable.

Operant behavior is somewhat different. Whether an operant behavior occurs is less a sure thing and more a function of probabilities—the interaction of multiple, competing, and often subtle, historical and current variables (including ongoing verbal evaluations). Thus, operant behavior is inherently more flexible and amenable to change in the present moment. For example, the respondent reaction of blushing may be impossible to control during a public presentation, but the related operant tendency to cut the speech short may be controlled, albeit with some difficulty. The person may finish the presentation while blushing and *wanting* to run and hide. Behaviorally, the importance of wanting is the experience of an operant tendency—the felt probability of behavior due to the salience of current and historical variables—but we do not have to do what we want, and, conversely, we may do all sorts of things that we do not want.

Perhaps more than anything else, BA asks clients to do what they do not want to do or feel like doing in the moment, to actively and knowingly approach unwanted emotional experiences. Thus, BA focuses on activating operant behavior in the context of accepting—rather than trying to directly change—ongoing respondent reactions. Colloquially, BA approaches the question of changing feelings from the "outside-in" rather than the "inside-out" (Martell et al., 2001; p. 63). Changing from the outside-in requires acceptance of what is "in" and acting according to a predefined plan, goal, or value while feeling whatever respondent reactions may be occurring. Thus, a certain level of acceptance is implicit in even the most simple activation assignments.

BA does not completely abandon an emotional change agenda (e.g., feeling better eventually) as do other acceptance approaches such as ACT. In other words, BA views short-term acceptance of emotional states as required for activation. However, this activation is explicitly aimed at increasing contact with diverse, stable sources of positive reinforcement in the service of decreasing aversive respondent reactions in the long term. Despite this caveat, the focus on mindfulness and acceptance characterizes BA as one of a group of relatively new psychotherapy approaches, all rooted in established behavioral principles and theory, labeled "third-wave" psychotherapies (Hayes, Follette, & Linehan, 2004), including ACT and DBT. In support of this focus, there is increasingly empirical support that acceptance interventions lead to greater tolerance of aversive emotional reactions and a greater willingness to engage in exposure to aversive stimuli than do direct efforts to stop the emotional reactions (Hayes, Luoma, Bond, Masuda, & Lillis,

2006) In other words, paradoxically, acceptance of aversive emotional reactions may in fact be the best strategy for reducing them.

THE DISTINCTIVE PRACTICAL FEATURES OF BEHAVIORAL ACTIVATION

15

A distinct structure

In Part 2 of this book we present the specific techniques of BA organized around a specific structure. As discussed in Point 1, there are several variants of BA, including BA (Martell et al., 2001) and BATD (Lejuez, Hopko, & Hopko, 2001), each emphasizing a different but overlapping set of techniques. Our goal with this book was to provide a cohesive structure that organized these techniques functionally while maximizing BA's efficiency, ease of implementation, and flexibility. The structure described herein provides (a) simple, powerful activation interventions very early in treatment, (b) a simple functional assessment strategy, consistent with the behavioral ABC model presented in Point 5, to be employed with clients for whom simple activation is not successful, and (c) additional specific BA techniques to be employed based on the ongoing results of functional assessment, allowing treatment to be tailored to the individual.

Figure 2 presents this overall structure and here we provide an overview of the subsequent points that describe these major BA techniques in more detail. We recommend that Session 1 includes standard history taking and discussion of the treatment rationale (Point 16), the assignment of initial activity monitoring (Point 17), initial values assessment (Point 18), and provision of a simple activation assignment (Point 19) if possible. This simple activation assignment is important to establish the active nature of BA, instill a sense of hope for the client, and maximize the possibility of early treatment gains, which are likely to happen after the first session (Busch, Kanter, Landes, & Kohlenberg, 2006).

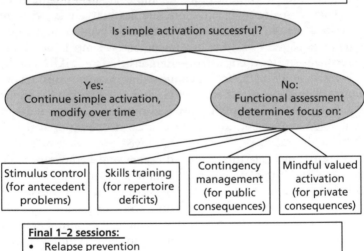

Session 1:
- History taking
- Provide rationale
- Begin activity monitoring
- Begin values assessment
- Simple activation assignment if possible

Sessions 2–4:
- Continue activity monitoring as necessary
- Complete values assessment
- Create activity hierarchy based on activity monitoring and values assessment
- Begin simple activation based on activity hierarchy

Sessions 3+:
- Continue simple activation
- Functional assessment based on success/failure with simple activation

Is simple activation successful?

Yes:
Continue simple activation, modify over time

No:
Functional assessment determines focus on:

Stimulus control (for antecedent problems)

Skills training (for repertoire deficits)

Contingency management (for public consequences)

Mindful valued activation (for private consequences)

Final 1–2 sessions:
- Relapse prevention

Figure 2 The structure of Behavioral Activation

In Session 2, the clinician continues activity monitoring if necessary, hopefully completes the values assessment (although this may last additional sessions), and creates an initial activity hierarchy based on what was learned from activity monitoring and values assessment. As discussed in Point 19, this activity hierarchy then guides simple activation for the next several sessions. Treatment focuses on simple activation (Point 19), reviewing simple activation homework assignments (Point 20), and functional assessment (Point 21) of success and failure of simple activation.

After these initial sessions, treatment becomes more flexible. Many clients will have experienced major gains simply through simple activation and treatment need not become more complicated (Hopko, Lejuez, Ruggiero, & Eifert, 2003). Functionally, we expect these clients to be those for whom depression was characterized by relatively easily identifiable behavioral reductions which led to losses of or reductions in contact with positive reinforcers, which are now potentially available in the environment. These clients will demonstrate relatively intact repertoires for contacting positive reinforcement once these repertoires are activated, and motivation to activate will not be complicated considerably by histories of negative reinforcement or punishment.

For example, Helen lost her job, moved to a new city where she did not have many friends, and became depressed. She then additionally stopped exercising, cleaning her house, and calling her old friends, and after a brief effort she stopped looking for new employment. Simple activation worked—Helen quickly became active after the first week of activation assignments, dancing (which she used to love) in her house daily for exercise, calling her old friends, and making local contacts for both social and employment purposes. Although she did not immediately make new friends and find a new job (this took several weeks longer), she immediately began to feel better and realized how her inactivity caused her to spiral into deeper and deeper depression.

Simple activation will not be sufficient for other clients, however. Thus, Point 21 describes how functional assessment of failed simple activation efforts during the first several sessions can lead to additional behavioral interventions as necessary, based on the behavioral ABC model. Specifically, stimulus control interventions (Point 22) target problems associated with antecedents for behavior, skills training interventions (Point 23) target problems associated with the behavioral repertoire itself, and contingency management (Point 24) and mindful valued activation (Point 25) interventions target problems with consequences (e.g., excessive positive or negative reinforcement for depressive behavior). Contingency management interventions focus on consequences in the external environment (e.g., a partner inadvertently punishes the depressed person for attempts to activate), while mindful valued activation interventions focus on consequences that are internal and private (e.g., reductions in anxiety that negatively reinforce avoidance behaviors). These more functional, flexible BA interventions may be applied over the course of treatment until the more tractable problems targeted by them show improvements. Finally, our approach to BA ends with relapse prevention strategies (Point 26).

The structure of a BA session

The typical BA session is structured to focus the clinician and client on concrete functional behavior change and in many ways is similar to a typical cognitive-behavioral therapy session (e.g., agenda setting, homework assignment and review, asking the client to summarize key points, asking the client for feedback on the session). BA sessions typically start with a review of the client's symptoms of depression (e.g., with a Beck Depression Inventory; Beck, Steer, & Brown, 1996). We also recommend the clinicians review the Behavioral Activation for Depression Scale (Kanter, Mulick, Busch, Berlin, & Martell, 2007; Kanter, Rusch, Busch, & Sedivy, in press), which was developed to measure the degree to which a client activates over the course of BA. The bulk of a BA session is spent reviewing the previous week's homework, devising new assignments, and problem solving potential barriers to the completion of new homework (Point 20). Specific, concrete homework review is, in essence, the way the BA clinician learns about the client and his or her life. The specific nature of the homework reviewed and assigned depends, of course, on where the client is in treatment and the functional assessment. The session typically ends with a brief review of the session, and at this time the clinician may ask the client for feedback on what was helpful and not helpful about the session.

16

The initial treatment rationale

In the first session, the BA clinician listens to the client's story and assesses for the environmental factors in depression discussed in Part 1. Ideally, towards the end of the session the clinician has enough of a behavioral conceptualization of the client's problems to present a summary and rationale for treatment that incorporates major elements of the story. The summary should highlight the major environmental components of the story and their emotional impact on the client to establish the therapist as empathic, validating, and supportive. The summary should be non-blaming and focus on depression as a normal human reaction to difficult and negative life events. The summary also establishes the activation assignments to follow. For example, the clinician may say:

> I have been listening to your story and I'd like to summarize what I've been hearing for a minute or two. Is that OK? Overall, I want to say that you really have gone through a lot and, in the context of everything you have and are going through, your depression makes complete sense to me. First, you mentioned how you broke up with your boyfriend, and it was not just the loss of the boyfriend, but you had really invested your hopes and dreams for the future into him, and these were lost too. Second, you mentioned how your parents just do not get who you are or what you need, and in fact your mom continually trying to push religion on you just makes you more distant. So, in an ideal world, you would have supportive parents, but in your world, that support is lost. Third, you talked about how you are struggling with school, how it is a constant source of stress for you, and

you don't really know why you are doing it or what you want out of your life. So you are not getting much meaning or enjoyment out of that.

Overall, I'm seeing a life that is filled with loss, conflict, and negatives, and not much positive. And when lives are this way, people feel the way you do. There is nothing broken in you for feeling this way, and you are not crazy or weak or defective. How you feel is how people feel when they have your life. Your depression makes perfect sense.

So we are going to figure out how to make your life meaningful and pleasurable again. The first thing we have to do is get you active and engaged in life, get you moving either towards your goals or moving towards figuring out what those goals are. Get you moving so you feel like you are starting to solve some of these problems. And get you moving simply so there is some fun and pleasure in your life again. How does this sound to you?

The BA clinician should also discuss with the client that BA is an empirically supported treatment approach which has been shown in scientific research to help the majority of individuals who receive it. In essence, the clinician seeks to instill hope and optimism in the client that the treatment makes sense and will work.

17

Activity monitoring

Activity monitoring has a long history as a behavior therapy assessment tool, but research suggests that it may be important to outcome on its own (Heidt & Marx, 2003). It is incorporated in both BA and BATD. We recommend that an initial activity monitoring assignment is given in Session 1, to begin obtaining detailed information about the frequency and patterns of specific client behaviors and the breadth or restriction of activity in general over time. The clinician and client should collaboratively determine the specific format of activity monitoring that will work best for the client. This can be the traditional activity chart (a simple day/time grid), a calendar or day planner, or a diary or journal (i.e., each night the client journals about his or her day), as long as it provides the clinician with the necessary information. In general, the client is asked to monitor activity and record it repeatedly over the course of the week, to get the most accurate record possible, but often clients will complete it nightly or just before the session, retrospectively. Any information collected is to be regarded as helpful by the therapist.

Why assign activity monitoring?

Activity monitoring provides relatively accurate information about the client's baseline functioning and level of activity. Establishing baseline functioning is important as both a comparison to functioning later in treatment and because the BA clinician seeks to assign graded homework that is likely to be completed successfully. Activity monitoring also can increase client awareness of his or her current activity level.

Most importantly, activity monitoring provides important information that informs the case conceptualization and leads to specific activation assignments. For example, if a client indicated in the first session that she often took long naps during the day that interfered with daily responsibilities, the clinician may ask that the client pay particular attention to events and emotions occurring near her naps. This client may return an activity chart that indicates that she often naps during the day when she is home alone and has been feeling lonely or bored. This information would suggest that for this client napping serves to avoid or escape loneliness or boredom and alternate activities could be assigned to decrease boredom at these times.

What should the client monitor?

Initial activity monitoring assignments often simply ask the client to track all behavior, hour-by-hour between sessions. Additional variables often related to depression can also be tracked, such as mood, mastery or pleasure ratings during each activity, using a simple rating scale such as 0 to 10. Alternately, the clinician may ask the client to note what mood he or she was in during the activity, which can be tailored to the sophistication of the client (e.g., happy, angry, sad, or anxious). Initial monitoring may lead to more specific behaviors to monitor, such as sleep, caffeine or alcohol use, time spent watching television or playing video games, time spent alone, or any other relevant variable.

Presentation of a fairly generic activity monitoring assignment may sound like the following:

> In order to gauge your current activity level and to get some ideas about why you are depressed, I would like to ask you to fill out this chart. As I don't know very much about what your days look like yet, I'd like to ask you to try to record as much of your day as possible. Record even those activities that might seem mundane or insignificant. One thing I would

like us to investigate is how your mood varies across different situations and activities, so I would like to have you rate your mood as well. Can you rate your mood on a scale of 0 to 10, with 0 representing low mood and 10 representing high mood, for each activity you record?

Roadblocks to activity monitoring

It is not uncommon for clients to view activity monitoring as childlike. This response can be mitigated by involving the client in deciding what is tracked and the format in which it is recorded. Reminders that activity monitoring only will occur for a few weeks, and that the information is very helpful to the clinician to get as accurate an assessment of baseline activity as possible, also are often helpful.

Paradoxically, a client who views activity monitoring as childlike may also experience it as too hard. This may be the case for clients who are particularly lethargic and inactive, as any increase in activity or attempt at establishing a routine will be experienced as difficult. For these clients, simply completing an activity chart is an activation assignment and it should be treated as such (see Point 19). Clients can be reminded that even partial progress will be helpful, and obstacles that may get in the way of completing it may be discussed.

For other clients, completing an activity chart may be shameful or embarrassing depending on the activities the client is or is not engaging in. For example, a client may be engaged in illegal behavior, not want to admit that he spent several hours watching pornography on the internet, or simply be embarrassed to admit that she did not get out of bed until late in the afternoon. It may take some time for such clients to develop a trusting therapeutic relationship with the clinician, but clinician reminders that any information is better than none, that the clinician will not judge the client for his behavior and the goal is to help the client, and that all information, even about illegal behavior, is confidential and protected (with the usual exceptions, explicitly spelled out to the client) may be helpful in speeding the process.

Some clients do not complete activity monitoring. This may be a result of multiple factors and should trigger functional assessment procedures as per Point 21. Other clients are *too* thorough at completing the activity monitoring assignment at the cost of avoiding other activities. For example, if a client spends an hour a day completing the activity monitoring form, this is too much time. Setting time limits for activity monitoring may be helpful. Another alternative for such a client is to complete the activity monitoring form for only two days during the week (e.g., one week day and one weekend day).

Reviewing activity monitoring

As with any assignment, it is essential that the clinician review the monitoring assignment in the following session and highlight its usefulness. It is often useful to first explicitly reinforce any attempt at monitoring. In general, monitoring forms should be scanned for activity deficits (e.g., never left the house), excesses (e.g., slept all day), and any relationship between mood and activity (e.g., mood was elevated when talking to a friend). This review should lead directly to individualized simple activation assignments.

A frequent difficulty we have encountered is when the clinician spends the whole session reviewing the client's self-monitoring homework and is unable to get to additional material. If this occurs, one option is to have the client complete the activity monitoring form every other week. If possible, the clinician may review the activity chart prior to the session while the client is completing paperwork in the waiting room, to enable a more structured review of the activity chart. Another alternative is to set a specific time limit to review activity monitoring, only reviewing the high points and low points of the week.

Monitoring behavior in the therapy relationship

As BA clinicians, we aim to be good behaviorists, and—behaviorally speaking—there is nothing more powerful than observing and intervening on live behavior, as it occurs during the clinical hour (Kohlenberg & Tsai, 1991). Thus, in addition to standard activity monitoring, the clinician always should be paying attention to the client's activity level during the therapy session (Kanter, Manos, Busch, & Rusch, 2008). For example, does the client show up on time to session? Make eye contact? Talk with pressure or in a slow monotone? Avoid difficult conversation topics? Appear to be falling asleep or having difficulty staying on topic? React with passivity to homework assignments? These observations may be incorporated with standard activity monitoring and values assessment to shape activity hierarchies and activation assignments.

18

Values assessment

The goal of BA is to produce contact with diverse, stable sources of positive reinforcement and create a life with meaning and purpose. This constructivist goal is not antithetical to symptom reduction, as depressive symptoms should be reduced through increased contact with positive reinforcement. It is, however, in a paradoxical relationship with symptom reduction, as our theory holds that symptom reduction is best achieved through the willingness to experience the very symptoms one hopes to reduce, as one activates in increasingly difficult areas of life. Therefore the targets of BA are not symptoms to be reduced, but alternative behaviors to be activated. In this Point we discuss values assessment as a method for determining these alternate behaviors and guiding activation assignments.

The importance of assessing the client's values as to guide activation assignments has been recognized by many BA authors (e.g., Gaynor & Harris, 2008; Lejeuz, Hopko, & Hopko, 2001; Martell et al., 2001; Veale, 2008). Steve Hayes and his colleagues first proposed values as an important behavior therapy tool and provided a full discussion of how to work with values as part of ACT (Hayes et al., 1999). Lejuez and colleagues (2001) provided a simple protocol that borrowed heavily from the ACT values assessment. The suggestions we provide here are based on Lejuez and colleagues' protocol and ACT, with some minor elaborations and adjustments.

Many clients find that discussions of values, and framing activation assignments in terms of those values, dignifies the process of activation by making it more meaningful. The protocol is simple and starts with a list of valued life areas. Although the specific life areas listed may be changed as appropriate by the clinician and client, below is a list we have employed, based on the Valued Living Questionnaire (VLQ) that was designed for ACT (Wilson et al., 2008). This list is:

- marriage, couples, intimate relations
- parenting
- other family relationships
- friendships, social relations
- employment, meaningful work
- education, training, life long learning
- recreation, hobbies, creative and artistic expression
- spirituality
- citizenship, community, activism, altruism
- physical well being, health, nutrition, self-care
- life organization, time management, discipline, finances
- other.

In Session 1, the clinician may present this list to the client as a homework assignment. The clinician may suggest that the client take a look at it and start to think about the areas of importance to him or her. In the subsequent sessions, the clinician and client work collaboratively to clarify these values and turn them into concrete behavioral goals. The following questions may be helpful in clarifying these values: (1) How have your actions been consistent with this value for the last week? (2) What type of person would you like to be in this area? (3) What immediate concrete goals related to this area can be defined? Through such questioning, the clinician and client together may define specific activation assignments related to the client's values and goals. This may be revisited as necessary over the course of therapy.

The VLQ (Wilson et al., 2008) also incorporates a process that we find helpful to BA. Specifically, clients are asked to rate how important each value is to them on a scale from 1 to 10, and also to rate how consistent their actions have been with each value over the last week (question 1 above) on a scale from 1 to 10. Observing discrepancies and consistencies between importance ratings and consistency ratings may be helpful to clients in structuring activation assignments.

Several considerations may be helpful in maximizing the success of this process. First, it is important to define values in a way that leads to activation assignments. As stated by Hayes and colleagues (1999), values are ideals and can never be fully achieved or totally satisfied. A salient metaphor for valuing is moving in a direction; you may keep going West, but you are never there. Thus, the most useful values are stated in a way that provides direction; specifically direction to activation assignments. Values also are most useful when they are stated in terms of the client's behavior, not in terms of the consequences of the client's behavior. For example, "I value being a good father" is better than "I value my children loving me" because the former is stated in terms of the client's behavior and can thus lead to more concrete goals and assignments. It may be helpful to view "valuing" as a behavior—something one does—to facilitate the translation of values into concrete behavioral goals. Thus, the client may be asked, "How did you value being a good father this week?"

Also, it is important to note that symptom reduction ("I value not being depressed") is not an acceptable value within the BA framework, nor is achieving any particular feeling state ("I value being happy" or "I value being relaxed"). The problem with a focus on feeling states, as we have already discussed, is that they come and go and are largely uncontrollable. Clients who state such values will need to be gently directed toward constructive behavioral values. For example, the clinician may say:

> I want you to be less depressed too, and our treatment hopefully will produce that. But we have learned that the best way to do that is to think about what your life would look like if you were depression free—what would you be doing with your family, your kids, your career? Then, I'm going to help you get moving in those areas without waiting

for your depression to go away. I know this sounds hard, maybe even impossible, but I promise you it isn't. The current step is to shift your focus away from these feelings and toward what you really want out of life.

Third, the list of potential values we have provided is quite specific. Various alternative ways of delineating values certainly could have been employed. The current list was created with the ultimate goal of concrete activation assignments in mind. Thus, valued domains were chosen that represented distinct and concrete life areas. Clients, however, may discuss values at different levels of abstraction. For example, Christine stated, "I value being a well-rounded person," and Bill stated, "I value being authentic." In Christine's case, the clinician suggested that the list of valued life domains was a way for Christine to think about how she wanted to be well-rounded. In Bill's case, the clinician suggested that they look at each valued domain as a context in which Bill could work on activating more authentic behaviors. Thus, as always in BA, the clinician's skill is in moving from the abstract to the concrete in ways that retain the deep meaning and purpose that clients desire from therapy experiences.

Difficulties with values assessment

Some depressed clients may report no values. For these clients, functional assessment procedures (Point 21) should be helpful in identifying the source of the problem. Some may simply have never thought about values (this would be a stimulus control problem, see Point 22). Others may resolutely insist on the futility of values. For these clients, it is likely that valuing, as a behavior, has been punished and extinguished. Years of struggle and failure may have resulted in hopelessness, and a potential discussion of values, hopes, and dreams will be a painful reminder that will be actively and persistently avoided. For other, possibly younger clients, negative interactions with and pressures from parents may have resulted in active avoidance of values and goals as a form of counter-control or a reaction to contingencies that established valued behavior as something that must be done for the parents, rather than something that can be done for oneself.

In both of these cases, values work will not be simple. Obviously, patience will be required and the work should be broken down into manageable parts. For example, if a client feels overwhelmed by the initial values assessment assignment, the clinician may suggest that they focus only on one or two areas. For other clients, values work at the beginning of therapy simply may be impossible, and the client's lack of ability to identify values should not stall activation assignments developed through other means. Delineation of values may be revisited later in therapy, after a client has achieved some activation and become more hopeful, and may be more successful at that point.

19

Simple activation

The most basic of BA interventions is simply assigning engagement in non-depressed behaviors between sessions to contact diverse, stable sources of positive reinforcement. Although a variety of techniques are included in BA and are discussed in this book, basic activity scheduling may in fact be the active ingredient that is responsible for BA's empirical success. If one examines the treatment components that have been included in all studies of behavioral therapies for depression, scheduling of non-depressed activities is the one constant (Cuijpers et al., 2007). Furthermore, the component analysis of CT by Jacobson and colleagues (1996) suggested that simple activation may be responsible for the empirical success of the whole CT package. Since that study, Jacobson and his colleagues developed a version of BA (Martell et al., 2001) that performed very well in a large randomized trial (Dimidjian et al., 2006). That version includes activity scheduling but also includes a primary focus on avoidance which may also be important, particularly for moderate to severely depressed clients.

In line with this reasoning, the current book presents a protocol that focuses on relatively unelaborated activity scheduling, which we term simple activation, and only steps up to more complicated interventions, such as focusing on avoidance, if simple activation fails. What we call simple activation is consistent with Martell and colleagues (2001) but largely follows Lejuez and colleagues (2001), who called for activity scheduling that is individualized based on an assessment of values and ongoing activity monitoring without more elaborate techniques. Essentially, the clinician integrates activation targets generated from activity monitoring with activation targets generated from values assessment to create an activity hierarchy. This hierarchy functions much like an exposure hierarchy does in exposure treatments for anxiety disorders (e.g., Franklin & Foa, 2008) by ranking activities in terms of difficulty. The goal is to generate a diverse set of activities across the full spectrum of difficulty level, such that the client may progress gradually and steadily up the hierarchy by completing increasingly difficult activities. In addition to simple activation being informed by activity monitoring and values assessment, the clinician should query for basic activities the client may have stopped doing (e.g., laundry, hygiene) and integrate these activities into the list as necessary.

Figure 3 presents a sample activity hierarchy, with items filled in after the first two weeks of therapy (a complete hierarchy would include blank rows to the bottom of the page, to allow additional activities to be noted as therapy proceeds). In addition to listing the activities, the hierarchy also contains a column for the client to list the anticipated difficulty of the activity, allowing the client and clinician to schedule them in a graded fashion. Columns for noting if and when the activity was assigned and completed are included. These can be used flexibly, depending on what makes the most sense and the preferences of the client. For example, some activities that are to be done daily may suggest a hash-mark system, while others simply may be noted with the date assigned and completed, a "yes" or a simple check mark. A final column for "actual difficulty" allows the client to assess how the difficulty of assignments may change over time.

The items on an activity hierarchy and their order are determined collaboratively with the client, and the clinician maintains sensitivity to what is likely to be successful for a client, and to issues of diversity and stability, as discussed in Point 7. For example, Michael, a 20 year old male who lived at home with his mother, revealed through activity monitoring that he spent almost all of his time at home and in fact rarely left his room during the day. Upon questioning about this,

Activity	Anticipated difficulty	Assigned	Completed	Actual difficulty
Get out of bed by 9 am	1	Yes	ⅢⅢ Ⅲ	1
Do the dishes 1/day	1	3/08/08	3/09/08	0
Take 20 min. walk	2	Yes	Yes	1
Call best friend 2/week	3	3/15/08	Ⅲ	2
Attend yoga 1/week	3			
Sign up for piano lessons	4	Yes	Yes	
Ask co-worker for help on 1 task/week	5			
Go to party, only talk to people you know	5			
Start conversation with 2 women at party	6			
Start conversation with 2 men at party	7			

Figure 3 A sample activity hierarchy

Michael revealed that he did not have a driver's license and relied on his mother for transportation. His value assessment revealed that he valued relationship intimacy, leading a purposeful life, and physical health, which led to treatment goals of finding an intimate relationship, finding a job and his own place to live, and engaging in more physical activity. It was clear to Michael and his clinician that his lack of a driver's license was restricting his ability to pursue some of his values, but Michael felt that studying for the licensing exam would be extremely difficult. Therefore, his activity hierarchy started with simple exercise (running) to increase his fitness. This assignment also simply got Michael out of the house regularly. Initial assignments also included going to the Department of Motor Vehicles to obtain study materials for the licensing exam, but not starting to study yet. Finally, initial assignments included going to a movie and playing his guitar.

In addition to the activity hierarchy, we also recommend the activation sheet to guide the scheduling of specific activities (Figure 4). Each simple activation assignment should explicitly detail the *who*, *what*, *where*, and *when* of activation (listed as *w/w/w/w* on the sheet). For example, Michael and his clinician determined that running for 20 minutes a day, three times a week, would be sufficient for the first week. Michael initially had proposed that he run every morning, but after discussion with his clinician he reduced this goal for the initial week to increase the likelihood of success. They also decided that he would exercise in the morning, at 10 am, as that would also serve to get him out of bed and hopefully provide him more energy for the day. They discussed if Michael had running gear and Michael said he already did. They also discussed a specific route for Michael to run that would be enjoyable.

The activation sheet can also be used to predict and prepare for unexpected events to which the client would like to respond differently. For example, based on valuing being a good mother, Cheryl wanted to respond with less anger when her two children were fighting with each other. This activity could not be

Activity homework				
Activity	w/w/w/w	Foreseeable obstacles	Solutions to obstacles	Outcome

Figure 4 A sample activation sheet

scheduled because it required her two children to fight, which was unpredictable. Thus, the clinician and Cheryl decided to include in the *w/w/w/w* column, "any time children are fighting" and in the *activity* column included, "attend to both children's needs equally."

Simple activation in the therapy relationship

The BA clinician should be constantly on the lookout for opportunities to develop in-session simple activation assignments. The benefit of such live assignments is that the clinician is present to control the consequences that follow improved client behavior. For example, Anna continually looks down, talks very softly and slowly, and appears disinterested in session. The clinician may say, "I'd like you to try to activate a little right now and act less depressed." If Anna does so successfully (even partially), clinician feedback is imperative, as in, "This is much better—I can understand you better and you're simply more enjoyable to be around." More important, however, is that the session actually becomes more productive and that Anna experience this improved session as due to her changed behavior.

Is simple activation enough?

Simple activation is, indeed, simple, and the reader may wonder if it is possible for such a simple technique to fully address such a complex problem as depression. Our answer is: It depends. We have seen simple activation succeed and fail. When it succeeds, it is generally because, after some initial successes with assigned activities, the client becomes active in a much broader sense, engaging in a myriad of additional activities that have not been scheduled specifically as activation assignments. In other words, the client responds to the overall rationale and assignments positively, learns very quickly that activation will be helpful, and this generalizes into multiple domains of the client's life as natural reinforcement for active behaviors takes hold. For these clients, only a handful of sessions will be required and later sessions can be shortened to brief homework check-ins.

With other clients, simple activation will not succeed, but this does not mean that it should not have been attempted. The lessons learned from the failure of simple activation become key factors in determining how to tailor the treatment more specifically to the individual client and overcome the obstacles that blocked simple activation. Thus, our protocol starts with simple activation, capitalizing on the power of this simple technique, maximizing the possibility of a quick recovery, and also providing necessary data for the functional assessment of activation problems that will guide treatment for those for whom simple activation fails. We recognize that some clinicians may observe functional deficits in the clients immediately suggesting that simple activation will fail, and prefer instead to move directly to more complex techniques such as mindful valued activation, which is more consistent with Martell BA. These clinicians may be right in such assessments but it remains an empirical question, so we prefer to start with the simpler techniques.

20

The importance of homework

All cognitive and behavioral therapies incorporate homework to a considerable degree, and in BA it is fundamental. Successful BA revolves around the assignment and completion of homework; every session should include some form of homework and BA is arguably not BA without homework. Some readers may be surprised at the time and energy BA clinicians devote to assigning, problem solving, and reviewing homework and the level of detail of these discussions. It is routine for these activities to take up a significant portion of sessions and later sessions may consist of little other than reviewing previous homework and assigning new homework.

Homework in BA usually has a simple purpose: To provide specific instructions to the client on the who, what, where, and when of activation assignments. Homework is the mechanism through which concrete talk, assessment of values, and construction of an activity hierarchy in the therapy session leads to contact with positive reinforcement in the outside world. Thus, when practicing BA, one can not spend too much time on homework. In general, homework assignments physically take the form of the activity hierarchy and activation sheet presented in the previous Point.

In general, it is important to develop homework assignments that have a good likelihood of success and are meaningful to a client. For example, if a client suggests that she clean the whole house between sessions and the clinician sees this as overly ambitious and likely to fail, the BA clinician should suggest a more reasonable activation assignment, such as cleaning one specific room. It is important, specifically early in treatment, to create client successes. Asking questions such as, "Does this seem like a reasonable task to complete in the next week?" or "Do you foresee yourself being able to complete this before next session?" can aid in setting the client up for success.

Particularly useful homework assignments may be ones that flow directly from in-session activation assignments. For example, Anna, discussed in the previous Point, may be given a homework assignment to continue to try to appear less depressed and more alert in interpersonal interactions, and be asked to observe how others respond to her differently. These homework assignments benefit from the client already having experienced at least one positive consequence to the assigned behavior in session with the clinician. Thus, the clinician knows that the client is capable of engaging in the behavior and has some sense for how others may respond, based on the clinician's assessment of his or her own natural response.

Barriers to homework completion

An initial consideration is that the term "homework" may be provocative for some clients, and the clinician should feel free to use whatever term is useful, such as "out-of-session practice" or "experiments."

To maximize the probability of success, it is essential that the BA clinician assess for barriers to homework completion. For some clients, this assessment can be as simple as asking, "What is going to stop you from doing X this week?" or "What are some reasons you might not be able to do this assignment?" It is important that the clinician does not ignore very simple barriers, such as simple forgetfulness, or being too tired, as these are often central issues for clients.

There are almost always barriers and clinicians should be skeptical if a client suggests none; this is usually a function of the client not thinking the assignment through rather than no barriers. For example, consider Amy who agreed to the activation assignment to attend her child's high school sporting event and who reported that she did not foresee anything that would get in the way of completion. Walking Amy through the steps necessary to follow through with her homework, however, revealed several potential obstacles, such as finding out where and when the next game was, buying a ticket, and finding transportation.

Once barriers have been identified each one should be problem-solved in session. For example, Amy and her clinician scheduled a time on the activity chart to investigate the schedule and buy a ticket. The clinician also asked Amy during the session to call the school to obtain the team's schedule. The clinician also could have worked with Amy to generate a list of transportation options and, if needed, addressed these issues in session as well (e.g., checking the bus schedule on-line during session).

It may be useful to frame feeling bad or feeling worse when preparing for or following an assignment as a barrier to completion. Consider Jeremy who agreed to an assignment involving having a difficult discussion with his spouse whom he had been avoiding. The clinician and Jeremy correctly predicted that he would feel nervous before starting the discussion and intense emotion during the discussion. The pre-discussion nervousness and *expected* emotional reaction can both serve as barriers to completion. We discuss assignments that are sensitive to these barriers in Point 25.

Homework review

Fully completed homework assignments are, of course, the ideal in BA but are rare. Typically, a client who fully completes all the homework can be expected to improve quickly and treatment generally will be uncomplicated. However, some clients may be overly focused on homework completion out of fear of disappointing the clinician or not being a perfect therapy client. For these clients, paradoxically, homework completion is a form of avoidance. This is not necessarily a bad thing, especially at the beginning of treatment, as anything that helps the client activate may be beneficial. If this persists over time, however, the clinician should be sensitive to the possibility that the client will become inactive shortly after the end of the therapy relationship. This is discussed more fully in Point 26 on ending therapy, and the strategies described in that Point may be employed earlier in therapy for these clients.

For most clients, however, partially completed homework assignments are the norm. In general, especially earlier in therapy, clinicians should be happy with any completed activity that is an improvement over the client's baseline. Clients, however, are often unhappy with their performance in these situations, largely because they are comparing their current performances to what others are doing or to what they were capable of before they became depressed. It may be useful for the clinician to highlight that the most relevant comparison is to the client's level of activity just before the assignment, not to some other criterion. It is easy for clinicians to think in terms of shaping in these situations, but harder for the client.

Clients sometimes interpret partial successes as total failures. However, in BA, the key is not how the client interprets the assignment, it is simply if activation was achieved and if the interpretation makes it less likely that activation will be sustained in the future. Thus, to a client who has interpreted partial success as complete failure, the clinician may suggest:

Given how depressed you have been, it makes perfect sense to me that you only completed some of the assignment. It also makes perfect sense to me that you are very self-critical about not completing more of it. The important point, for me, is that you are more active this week than you were last week. I think that is terrific. Do you think you can improve just a bit more next week, and we'll see what happens to your self-critical thoughts then, as you continue to improve?

With this response, the BA clinician stays focused on the primary issue, activation, acknowledges the client's negative thinking and does not get distracted by it. Notice also how the clinician's response implies that the client may *have* the negative thinking *and* continue to activate.

The review of homework assignments at the beginning of each session also should include a discussion of what prevented clients from completing homework or what barriers the client worked around to complete the assignment.

Staying concrete

The focus on homework also highlights a related theme in BA— the importance of staying concrete. Maintaining this focus requires continual monitoring of how behavior and homework are talked about in the therapy session. Consider the following interaction:

Client: Last week was a bad week. I just stayed in bed the whole time and didn't do my homework.

Clinician: You do seem really depressed this week. We really need to figure out how to get you out of bed and get you active again.

Client: I know I do. It is just so hard—I feel like my whole body is just screaming at me to stay in bed. I'm just so miserable, I feel like I'll never have a life again.

Clinician: Wow. It really is hard to activate when you're feeling that way. But I feel confident that if you get active, you'll start to build the life you want.

On the one hand, this interaction sounds like BA. The client is focused on her inactivity, and the clinician emphasizes activation. The clinician is also very empathic and validating, while at the same time encouraging activity.

But the conversation is quite abstract. They are discussing staying in bed and activation, but are discussing it in broad terms. We do not have a sense yet of the function of the client's behavior, and we do not have concrete examples of the behavior. If the conversation remained at this level of abstraction, it would be *talking about* BA but would not be BA. Such talking about BA is very appropriate at the beginning of treatment and throughout, as it is necessary to discuss the overall rationale for treatment and for specific treatment assignments with the client, and to have the client understand and agree with these rationales (Addis & Carpenter, 1999). The bulk of the work of BA, however, is much more concrete and specific than this.

Consider an alternative to the above interaction:

Client: Last week was a bad week. I pretty much just stayed in bed the whole time and didn't do my homework.

Clinician: You do seem really depressed this week. We really need to figure out how to get you out of bed and get you active again. Can we spend a few minutes on this?

Client: Sure.

Clinician: Good. First, you said you were in bed the whole week, but you must have gotten out of bed a few times, including coming to this session. Tell me about those.

Client: Well, I got out of bed earlier on Tuesday, and I made it here this morning.

Clinician: That's right, you are here right now, and I'm really glad you are. How did you manage that?

Client: I just forced myself, I guess.

Clinician: Well, let's figure this out. What time did you get up? How long did you lie in bed after your alarm went off? Did you consider canceling our appointment?

In this alternative, the clinician has first identified a specific instance of the behavior, and then has begun a line of questioning to understand the function of that behavior in detail.

Such detailed concrete analyses of homework assignments, and their success and failure, are the heart of BA, as they will lead to more specific and focused interventions.

21

Functional assessment

As discussed in Point 5, functional assessment requires a detailed understanding of the sequence of antecedent events that prompted the behavior of interest, the actual form of the behavior, and the consequences that followed the behavior. A good functional assessment requires the client to describe this sequence in detail, so the clinician may come as close as possible to observing the actual sequence. It requires an appreciation of subtle functional distinctions and the creativity, in the moment, to develop questions to ask to the client that will help the clinician make these distinctions.

Although extolled as fundamental to behavior therapy by behavioral clinicians, specific guidelines for how to conduct functional assessment for adult, outpatient populations were lacking for many years. BA is a case in point. Lejuez and colleagues (2001) described depression in functional terms but provided a very structured protocol that did not capitalize on the flexible, idiographic nature of functional assessment. Martell and colleagues (2001) did suggest functional assessment as a strategy, and specifically suggested that it was important to teach clients to conduct their own functional assessments, but this assessment largely was limited to avoidance repertoires and did not assess the full range of functional problems related to depression.

Some suggestions for functional assessment for adult outpatients have been provided by FAP (Kanter, Weeks, Bonow, Landes, Callaghan, & Follette, in press). These suggestions focus on how the clinician may observe and assess client behavior as it occurs in the therapy relationship, to help develop hypotheses about similar behavior occurring outside of therapy.

As we discuss below, BA assessment instead focuses directly on out-of-session behavior, but the good BA clinician should be sensitive to in session behavior, what is occurring functionally between the clinician and client, and how this relates to client out-of-session problems. A full functional assessment integrates what the clinician observes live with what the client reports about his or her outside behavior.

Possibly the best example of functional assessment for adult outpatients comes from DBT (Linehan, 1993), which was designed for multi-problem clients with Borderline Personality Disorder and other disorders of emotional regulation. We strongly encourage clinicians to learn DBT. However, DBT is quite complicated and requires long hours of training and supervision to achieve competence. Although necessary for the complex presentations for which it was designed, it may be more than is necessary for most depressed clients.

DBT's version of functional assessment is termed *chain analysis* or *behavioral analysis*, and it requires the clinician to question the client in detail about the chain of events surrounding the behavior of interest. This questioning leads to specific interventions. The current version of functional assessment described here owes considerable debt to Linehan's version. The goal here was to create a simple assessment procedure, tailored for outpatient depression, that could be quickly learned and applied in an outpatient setting.

This Point attempts to organize the available BA interventions into functional categories according to the behavioral ABC model and provides a simple method of functional assessment to guide the choice of intervention. The key is that therapy starts with simple activation and then, if simple activation does not succeed, the clinician employs this functional assessment to understand why simple activation did not succeed. Thus, functional assessment is to be incorporated into homework review when the assignment was not completed and suggests which, or which combination, of the available BA interventions should be employed. This sequenced protocol therefore gives simple activation, which requires less clinician training and functional understanding, a chance to succeed and only proceeds to more complex interventions as necessary. Put differently, simple activation culls the less complicated clients who will benefit from a simple approach, and then functional assessment allows for the tailoring of treatment to unique client characteristics for the clients who will require such tailoring.

Our strategy for functional assessment focuses on problems with antecedents (linked to stimulus control interventions), behavioral repertoire deficits (linked to skills training interventions), and consequences. Consequences are further divided into consequences that can be manipulated in the environment (linked to contingency management interventions) and consequences that are largely private events experienced by the client (linked to mindful valued activation interventions). These private consequences typically result in negatively reinforced avoidance behavior, which can take many forms including both deficits (e.g., staying in bed, not answering the phone) and excesses (e.g., shopping, being on the internet for long periods, comfort eating, masturbation). In this way, the full range of functional behavioral problems is captured by the assessment process and the full arsenal of BA techniques can be employed strategically. Although this sounds quite complex, in fact it is relatively simple and can be learned quickly in this Point and Points 22 to 25. Each functional category will be summarized here, including sample functional assessment questions. Interventions to address these categories will be explored in more depth in the next four Points.

A (antecedents): Deficits in stimulus control

The most common excuse for incomplete simple activation assignments is undoubtedly that the client simply forgot. Behaviorally, we refer to this type of forgetting as a deficit in stimulus control. Specifically, this means that the client's environment was not arranged to evoke the target behavior (i.e., activation).

Deficits in stimulus control are not hard to assess, and primarily consist of asking the client if he or she remembered to do the assignment.

Consider a clinician who asks the client, "How many times throughout the week did you think about completing the assignment?" If the client answers, "I thought about how I was going to complete the assignment in the car on the way home from last session, but it has not crossed my mind since then," stimulus control is probably a problem. Similarly, the client may respond, "I remembered in the shower in the morning, but then I forgot all day," or "I remembered while I was driving to work one morning." In these instances, remembering to do the assignment is occurring at the wrong times and this may also be seen as a deficit in stimulus control. However, if the client says, "I thought about doing my assignment for the first five days after last session, but I kept procrastinating because I was too tired and eventually forgot," the problem is more likely one of competing contingencies (consequences). Stimulus control interventions are reviewed in Point 22.

Questions to ask include:

- Did you decide against doing the assignment, or did you simply forget?
- How many times throughout the week did you think about completing the assignment?
- Did you remember to do the assignment at a time you would have been able to do it or at other times?
- Did you do anything concrete to help you remember? If so, what? Why do you think it didn't work?
- Which of the things you did to help you remember worked and which ones didn't?

B (behaviors): Repertoire deficits

Failed simple activation assignments often reveal that the client does not possess the skills necessary to complete the assignment.

Skill deficits become more relevant to assess as the activation assignments become more complicated. For example, for a severely depressed but cognitively intact client, simple hygiene (brushing teeth and taking a shower) may be activated, and we may assume the client possesses the requisite skills. However, a client who recently bought a house with a yard may be activated to plant a flower garden. While the client is excited about the prospect of this activity, she has always lived in a high rise apartment and knows little about gardening. In this case, initial assignments would focus on building gardening skills (e.g., buying and reading a gardening book) rather than on increasing immediate contact with positive reinforcement.

Skills deficits may be broken down into non-social skills and social skills. Questions to ask to assess non-social skills deficits include:

- Have you successfully done this kind of thing before, or was this really new for you?
- Did you have a good idea of what you needed to do before you started?
- What types of things did you do to plan or prepare for the assignment?
- Did you get started on the assignment and later get stuck? If so, on what?

A broad non-social skill that may be a focus of clinical attention is problem solving. For example, many clients, especially those struggling with poverty, find themselves overwhelmed by a laundry list of demands that compete with activation assignments, such as childcare obligations, children or elderly parents with special needs, medical appointments, government program appointments, time constraints due to public transportation, and making sure the bills are paid and the electricity is on and the phone is not disconnected. Such a client may be helped by learning skills related to organization, planning, scheduling, and problem solving. Questions to ask here include:

- Were you unable to complete the assignment because of these other obligations?
- How organized are your days? Do you have a scheduler or day planner?
- Were there times when you simply don't know what to do or how to prioritize everything?
- When you know you are going to be very busy, what types of things do you do to get organized?
- Do you find the demands of trying to do our assignments unrealistic given all of the time consumed on your other day to day responsibilities?

Trickier to assess are social skills, such as having a conversation with one's spouse, saying no to a friend making a request, responding to one's daughter without anger, or asking one's boss for a raise. It is easy for a clinician to overestimate a client's ability in these situations. Such complex interpersonal behaviors that are relatively easy and natural to the clinician, however, may be surprisingly hard for a depressed client. Questions to ask include:

- Did you feel like you knew what to say in the interaction?
- Did you feel that others heard or understood what you said?
- Did you feel confident when you spoke to him? Did you make good eye contact? How did you sit?
- Can you talk me through what you did, exactly what you said and how you said it, and how your partner/co-worker/friend reacted, so I can gauge what happened?

When assessing for repertoire deficits, the clinician must not mistake possible rumination (e.g., "I thought all week about what would be the best situation to approach him and the best words to use, but never ended up doing anything") or emotional avoidance (e.g., "I was going to talk to my boss, but I could not think of how to do it in a way that I would not be nervous") for a lack of skill. Furthermore, it is important to note that in some instances a client may have been extremely skillful and still could not obtain the desired outcome. For example, Lisa may have asked assertively and appropriately for time off of work and her boss did not fulfill the request because of other variables (e.g., a deadline is approaching and no employees are being given time off). Thus, it is important to distinguish between repertoire deficits and uncontrollable environmental variables that caused the activation assignment to result in an undesired outcome. Skills training interventions for correcting repertoire deficits are reviewed in Point 23.

C (consequences): Environmental consequences

Failure to activate as assigned is often caused (at least in part) by the reactions of others to the depressed individual. Specifically, family and friends of the client often unintentionally support depressed behaviors. Staying in bed and crying can evoke sympathetic gestures and prolonged attention from others (providing positive reinforcement) and/or can cause others to relieve the client of responsibilities (providing negative reinforcement). Punishment can also have a role in maintaining depressed behavior. For example, getting out of bed may be punished by a nagging spouse. This environmental support of depressed behavior (e.g., staying in bed) interferes with the completion of the non-depressive activation assignment (e.g., getting out of bed before noon).

Questions to assess environmental consequences focus on understanding the reactions of others. The examples focus on a spouse but can be modified for any interaction partner. Questions include:

• How did your spouse react when you did that? Is that reaction typical?
• Does your spouse generally react that way to people?

- If you were to do this assignment, how do you think your spouse would respond?

C (consequences): Private consequences

One of the contributions of Martell and colleagues' (2001) BA is its recognition of the importance of negative reinforcement for avoidance behavior. This avoidance is often intrapersonal—that is, the stimuli being avoided are internal experiences (i.e., aversive thoughts or feelings). For example, a client may avoid exercise because it causes them physical discomfort (e.g., shortness of breath) or a student may avoid talking to a professor about making up a missed assignment because it brings up aversive thoughts of being an inadequate student. While experiential avoidance and escape is quite natural, it serves to complicate simple activation assignments as it presents an ever present competing contingency against activation.

Assessing the role of experiential avoidance is harder than the other categories and in some ways can be arrived at through a process of elimination of the other categories. In other words, if stimulus control, skills deficits, and environmental consequences have been ruled out, it may be assumed that private consequences are relevant.

It also may be the case that a client is unable to specify why he or she did not do an assignment, and in this situation we would suspect experiential avoidance played a role as well. For example, Elena was asked to spend the day cleaning her apartment, but instead slept through most of the day. When asked what happened, she replied, "I don't really know, my alarm went off and I remembered I had to get up and clean but I just couldn't—I kept drifting in and out of sleep and never really woke up." For Elena, the consequences of getting out of bed were aversive compared to staying in bed; thus staying in bed was negatively reinforcing by successful avoidance of how she would feel if she got out of bed. The fact that Elena has little insight into this negative reinforcement process, and therefore cannot accurately report on it, makes it tricky for the clinician to discern

It is important to keep in mind when assessing private consequences that the client may have successfully avoided the private experience you are assessing. For example, Elena's clinician asked her, "Were you feeling anxious about getting up and doing the housework?" and Elena replied, "No, I wasn't feeling anything." Elena is not lying here and she is not "out of touch" with her emotions. Instead, we would suggest that Elena successfully avoided the experience of anxiety by staying in bed. Avoidance works! Thus, a better question for Elena would be, "Think about getting up and getting out of bed, putting your clothes on, and going downstairs to start the housework. How would you feel?" In this situation, the clinician has presented the cues for anxiety that Elena may have been successfully avoiding, so the clinician is more likely to get a response from Elena that will help the clinician decide if anxious avoidance was salient to the situation. Mindful valued activation interventions to address private consequences are reviewed in Point 25.

Often, problems with experiential avoidance and skills deficits go hand in hand. A client who is unskilled at an assigned activity will be more anxious about it, and more likely to avoid due to both the lack of skill and the anxiety. Thus, both skills training and mindful valued activation interventions may need to be employed. For example, consider Jill, a client in poverty, overwhelmed by daily survival demands, who may benefit from planning and organizational skills training. Yet, no matter how organized or how skilled she becomes at solving problems, severe problems related to being in poverty will remain.

In this situation, Jill will never complete activation assignments unless she learns how to cope with difficult emotions when diverting her energies to long-term goals (e.g., allow herself to feel the stress that comes from NOT always focusing on immediate survival). Often, activation requires individuals to focus on tasks that only in the long term will translate into gain, and Jill will feel many negative private consequences by spending time on activation assignments because they prevent her from focusing on daily survival

Questions to guide the clinician toward this category focus on the presence of strong emotional reactions, such as feeling exhausted, overwhelmed, or anxious. Questions include:

- Did you stop doing the activity because you were feeling frustrated, angry, stressed, or something similar?
- Do you think you avoided the activity because the idea of it was too stressful or something similar?
- How did you feel when you thought about/attempted this activity?
- What type of thoughts or emotions did you have about this activity?
- What was going on in your body at the time (anxiety, aches, etc.)?
- Did you think about doing the activity, and then abruptly start thinking about something unrelated?
- Did you consider completing the assignment, but then start doing other less important things (e.g. watching TV) until you eventually ran out of time to start the assignment?
- How would you feel if you were asked to set aside time away from things that need to be done NOW for things that will only help you in the near future?
- What wouldn't get done next week if you had done the assignment? What would you have felt if it didn't get done?

General considerations

Our delineation of functional categories was designed to high-light the *most salient* aspects of the behavior, functionally defined, that if addressed should result in successful activation. Thus, antecedent problems ideally are defined when a successful manipulation of environmental discriminative stimuli will be sufficient to produce the target activation behavior in the absence of repertoire or reinforcer changes. Repertoire problems ideally are defined when a successful skills training intervention will be sufficient to produce the target activation behavior in the absence of discriminative stimuli or reinforcer changes. Likewise, environmental consequence problems ideally are defined when a successful manipulation of environmental reinforcers through a contingency management intervention will produce the target activation behavior in the absence of other changes.

Problems with private consequences, however, are more complicated, and mindful valued activation interventions actually target several terms of the ABC model. Because private consequences are difficult to change, the goal of this activation is to decrease the salience or strength of aversive private stimuli through mindfulness interventions and to generate alternate behaviors maintained by verbally constructed consequences (statements of values) that will successfully compete with the immediate, private consequences that have maintained the problematic avoidance behaviors in the past.

Of course, it is often the case that obstacles to activation will surface in multiple domains. In other words, the four functional categories described above are non-orthogonal—a single failure to complete a simple activation assignment could be controlled by any number of these problems. For example, a client may put off an assignment because it made her anxious (private consequence) and eventually forget (deficit in stimulus control). Likewise, engaging in an intense discussion with one's spouse may produce a significant amount of anxiety (private consequence) because the client lacks the necessary interpersonal skill to conduct the discussion successfully (repertoire deficit). The interventions described in the next four Points provide techniques to address all of these issues, both alone and in combination.

22

Post-it notes and other stimulus control procedures

As mentioned above, clients often fail to complete homework at least partially due to forgetfulness. An assignment is designed in session, the client goes home for a week and forgets the assignment, and then returns the following session, perhaps remembering the assignment on the way to the appointment in the car. To a BA clinician, this is not an issue of laziness or lack of motivation to engage in therapy—it is an issue of stimulus control. The question for the BA clinician when confronted with a problem of stimulus control is how to arrange the client's environment in such a way that it will evoke the target behavior. Technically, stimulus control interventions insert somewhat artificial prompts (discriminative stimuli) into the client's environment in the hopes of evoking the target behavior at a higher rate.

In practice, stimulus control prompts often simply take the form of a sticky note, and the therapeutic skill is in determining where to put it. Post-it notes often are utilized as they are cheap, portable and can be advantageously placed. In addition, a family member can be asked to provide verbal reminders, or the clinician can volunteer to call with a reminder him or herself. If a clinician suspects that the client might not follow through with creating a prompt, one can be produced in session by having the client leave a recorded reminder on his or her own voicemail. Other creative and activity-specific stimuli can also function as powerful prompts. For example, if a client is assigned to walk the dog upon returning from work (perhaps to prevent the client from immediately turning on the television), the clinician might ask the client to hang the dog's leash on the outside of their entry door as a prompt.

The location of the prompt (i.e., where to put the note) is important. Should it go on the refrigerator, on the bedside table, on the bathroom mirror, on the car steering wheel, in the wallet, or on the cell-phone? All locations are not created equal, and the goal is to arrange the client's environment to cue the right behavior at the right time. If the client's goal is to call a friend, the note could be placed on her phone. If the assignment is to get dressed each day (as opposed to wearing pajamas all day) a note could be placed on the inside of the bedroom door. The importance of location also applies to non-written prompts. For example, if a client is laying out her gym clothing, the clothing should be placed where it will be seen immediately upon waking up. Similar considerations should be made regarding prompts consisting of reminders from others. It is important to consider when, and in what situations, it would be most useful for the client to receive a verbal reminder of their assignment.

Collaboration with the client is important in determining both the form and the context in which the prompt is presented, because clients often suggest poor stimulus control ideas. For example, some young clients may want to write the assignment "work out every morning this week" on their hand. This is a poor prompt for two reasons. First, the writing will inevitably be unreadable in a few days and unnoticeable before the end of the week. Second, this prompt is not tied to the behavior in any way, because the client may not glance at her hand more often during opportune times to work out.

We focus on stimulus control procedures as responses to initial failures of activation, but it should be noted that in some ways stimulus control interventions are built into basic activation assignments. For example, simply writing an assignment on an activity chart and discussing where the client will keep the chart itself is a basic stimulus control intervention. Likewise, calendars or day planners are common place and useful if the client already has an established routine of using them effectively. If not, learning this skill may be thought of as a repertoire problem (Point 23). An initial assignment to buy a planner may be useful.

A final consideration regarding stimulus control procedures is whether they are temporary measures that can be removed after a client is back on track or permanent changes that can help the client build a long term non-depressed routine. Some specific interventions mentioned above are clearly temporary (e.g., verbal reminders from friends), while others could be more permanent with minimal burden (e.g., keeping a calendar). Clients may feel that stimulus control interventions are childish, suggest that they require remedial training, or suggest that they simply lack willpower so it is important to explain to the client that prompts are necessary to evoke new behavior for everyone. Although we do not recommend a house covered in Post-it notes, in general as behaviorists we do appreciate the importance of regular prompts being built into one's permanent routine.

23

Skills training

Skills training is a widely used cognitive behavioral technique incorporated into a variety of treatment packages (e.g., Beck et al., 1979; Linehan, 1993). It is not unique to BA. These treatment packages, however, present skills training as a programmed component, whereas BA as presented here, consistent with Martell and colleagues (2001), does not recommend skills training for all clients. Instead the application of skills training in BA is contingent upon determining the presence of repertoire deficits through a functional assessment of failed simple activation assignments.

Here we present descriptions and examples of how to address non-social and social skill deficits. The brevity of the current descriptions should not suggest that skills training interventions are necessarily brief. Learning a new skill takes time, practice, trial and error. Clinician sensitivity to issues of shaping and reinforcing successive approximations to the desired level of skill is important, and providing this rationale to the client will be helpful. An analogy to a well-known skill, such as learning to play a piano or skiing, especially one that the client has developed, that clearly required patience, practice and a sequence of improvements to obtain may be helpful in setting the stage for a prolonged skills training intervention.

Non-social skills deficits

As an example of non-social skills deficits, consider Mary who is unemployed and does not know how to use online job search resources. Spending several sessions providing Mary a tutorial on computer use would be an inefficient use·of the clinician's time, so it may be more effective to refocus out-of-session activation assignments on obtaining the necessary skills. In this example, these assignments could involve attending a basic internet skills class or checking out a computer skills training book from the local library. Assignments could also focus on obtaining access to a computer in order to practice and apply these skills. Thus a non-social skills deficit often dictates that the clinician step back and assign activation assignments that will build the skills necessary.

Another particular skill that may need to be taught for some clients, especially those with overwhelming daily life stressors, may be problem solving. We recommend the simple framework for problem solving provided by Nezu, Nuzu, and Perri (1989).

Social skills deficits

Conversely, social skills deficits are more amenable to direct clinician manipulation. Social skills training is a therapeutic intervention that focuses on developing interpersonal skills that are both appropriate and effective (Sergin, 2003). We will provide a brief description and example of social skills training here and encourage further reading. We are particularly impressed with the skills training procedures of DBT (Linehan, 1993), which were originally designed for multi-problem clients with Borderline Personality Disorder but can be adapted for depressed clients.

As per Sergin (2003), social skills training can be broken into four components: (1) direct instruction on what to do differently, (2) modeling by the clinician of what improved performance looks like, (3) role-playing the target skill with clinician feedback, and (4) assignment of real world practice as homework.

Consider Jeremy, who has been planning a vacation, but has been unable to effectively request time off of work from his supervisor. Jeremy's clinician has identified that Jeremy has a repertoire deficit in making assertive requests to authority figures. After assessing this deficit, Jeremy's clinician presented didactic information about how Jeremy's requests could be improved (e.g., increased persistence and clarity). Then Jeremy's clinician modeled making an assertive request, followed by a role-play where the clinician played Jeremy's boss and Jeremy repeatedly practiced asking for time off. Between each role-play Jeremy's clinician provided feedback on what he did well and pointed out alternatives to what he did ineffectively. Finally, Jeremy was assigned to engage in assertive requesting outside of session. As with all assignments in BA, assignments should be carefully graded to improve the likelihood of success, and this process may take several weeks. For example, Jeremy's clinician asked him to test out his new skills on another, less intimidating authority figure in his life prior to asking his boss for vacation time.

Social skills training in the therapy relationship

We have been highlighting therapeutic opportunities to observe and shape more active, healthy behavior as it occurs live, in the therapy relationship, as per FAP. Repertoire deficits are prime examples of this, because if a client lacks or is weak at a certain interpersonal skill this often will be observed by the clinician in interaction with the client. The therapy relationship is a useful setting to shape and build such skills because the clinician may be more sensitive to partial improvements than others in the client's life. For example, consider a client who has great difficulty talking about how she feels. An initial, halting, awkward attempt at this may be a big improvement for the client, but its awkwardness may result in others punishing it or at least not responding positively. The clinician, who is sensitive to shaping approximations to ideal behavior, may be thrilled at such an initial, awkward attempt, and respond in fashion. The clinician also may tell the client that although she responded well to it personally, more practice in session is needed before the client may be ready to try it with others.

Focusing on live opportunities to shape interpersonal skills, however, may at times suggest interventions *opposite to* standard social skills training procedures. Again consider Jeremy as an example of a client with difficulty being assertive. The clinician, in fact, may represent an authority figure who specifically functions as an antecedent for passive, unassertive behavior. When the clinician suggested to Jeremy that they role-play a more assertive interaction with his boss, Jeremy replied, "I hate role-plays and I'd really prefer not to do this." The clinician now had a choice to either continue to encourage the role-play or to listen to Jeremy. Of primary importance here is that *Jeremy's statement about not wanting to role-play assertiveness actually is a very assertive statement.* Thus, the clinician may choose to not engage in role-play in this situation, in an effort to provide natural reinforcement for Jeremy's assertive behavior. In general, a somewhat paradoxical rule applies here for the clinician: When the clinician does not want to grant the request of an unassertive client, the very experience of not wanting to grant the request may be an indicator that the client is engaging in assertive behavior and the request should be granted. This is a tricky therapeutic move and additional considerations are provided in FAP texts by Kohlenberg and Tsai (1991) and Tsai et al. (2008).

24

Contingency management

When it is determined that simple activation has failed due to a lack of environmental support the BA clinician turns to contingency management procedures. Contingency management procedures traditionally have been defined as very systematic, supervised interventions that control the delivery of consequences following easily measurable target outcomes (e.g., weight loss, abstinence from alcohol). Although consequences provided in these programs are often quite arbitrary (e.g., money provided for drug abstinence), they have the advantage of establishing competing contingencies to work against entrenched problem behaviors and have been found to be quite effective (e.g., Melin, Andersson, & Götestam, 1976).

We use the term *contingency management* to refer to any attempt by the BA clinician to arrange contingencies to support out-of-session activation. Specifically, our discussion of contingency management is consistent with procedures developed by Lejuez et al. (2001) and focuses on contracting with significant others in the client's life to interact with the client in such a way that serves to increase non-depressed behavior. If successfully applied, contracting with significant others provides the most natural and immediate shaping of non-depressed behavior; however, it also requires that an appropriate individual is available, willing, and able to fulfill a contract and has control of salient contingencies. Thus, in many situations where environmental consequences are an issue, including when there is little natural reinforcement (interpersonal or otherwise) available or immediate action is necessary, interpersonal contracting is not a viable intervention. Other temporary contingency management procedures can be applied in these situations and are discussed below.

Contracting with significant others

Very simply, contracting with others in BA consists of specifying that significant others in the client's life will change how they react to the client's depressed (e.g., staying in bed) and non-depressed (e.g., getting out of bed) behavior in such a way that they stop reinforcing depressed behavior and start reinforcing non-depressed behavior. Significant others often help to maintain depression through well intentioned and loving responses to the depressed individual. These problematic responses may take the form of doing extra chores, excusing behavior that is typically not excused, or not making requests that are typically made. For example, consider Steve who recently lost his job and is currently going through a divorce. Steve stays in bed all day and has not been looking for new employment. Steve's apartment is a mess as he makes no effort to clean. As a result Steve's mother goes to his apartment and cleans thoroughly every week. Although Steve's mother is clearly doing her best to be supportive of her son, she is actually reinforcing Steve's depressive behavior (i.e., staying in bed and not doing chores). In fact she is actually preventing Steve from coming into contact with the consequences of his inactive behavior.

Ideally Steve's mother could be brought into session to discuss how she might react differently to Steve. The clinician can then present the BA rationale and explain why doing these behaviors may not actually be helping Steve become less depressed. It is important to be sensitive to the significant other's reaction to being told that their sensitive, loving responses may not always function as the response that will help the client. In the example above, Steve's mother viewed her behavior as loving and caring and it is often very difficult for family members to not behave in this way. If both the client and significant other are on board with the rationale, the clinician can present them with possible alternative responses to the client's behavior. For example, Steve's mother could be asked to not clean unless Steve is at least awake, out of bed, and helping with the cleaning. If he does help her, she could agree to do something he enjoys with him. Given the complexity, it is often helpful to write out a specific contract that can be signed and later referenced by either party. Contracts should be very specific. Each party should know what they are agreeing to and the consequences of following through or not.

Contracts can be effectively applied in a variety of situations and need not be complex. For example, a roommate could agree not to ridicule a client's initial attempts at a workout program, a spouse could agree to make dinner if the client spends the extra time filling out job applications, or a friend could agree to spend more time with a client if that time is not spent isolated in the client's apartment.

Other contingency management interventions

There are times in therapy when arbitrary contingency manipulations are needed to return the environment to a baseline that has been disrupted by prolonged depressed behavior or to support temporary but important activation assignments. Consider the mundane but necessary task of doing laundry. A depressed client may have put off doing laundry for several weeks, leaving a tremendous pile of dirty clothing that may take all day to wash, clean, fold, and put away. Completion of this task will probably not produce significant reinforcement and may be difficult to link to relevant values. Thus, the BA clinician may introduce a contingency that does not naturally occur in order to bring the task back to a manageable size that can be more successfully integrated into a routine (e.g., doing one load every Sunday). For example, the client could restrict television watching until she has completed the laundry, and then allow herself to watch television as a reward, or she would treat herself to a dinner out after completing the laundry. This self-administered reinforcement can also be written as a contract and signed by the client.

If this client watches television often, the first assignment above would be taking advantage of what is known as the *Premack Principle*—that a high frequency behavior may be employed as a reinforcer for completion of a lower frequency behavior. Put less technically, it is offering a "treat" for doing something hard. In general, BA clinicians are wary of using this principle (or other "treats" such as a dinner out), because the reinforcers are arbitrary and typically do not generalize well. The current example suggests when such an intervention may be necessary—when the behavior is important and unlikely to occur without such an arbitrary move. In such cases it may help kick start a long-term activation plan. In this case, after washing the backlog, doing a load of laundry could be scheduled at a specific time each week as an activation assignment.

It is important to note that artificial contingencies, including contracts, can be arranged between the client and the clinician when natural reinforcement is unavailable. Consider a client who enjoys having discussions and telling the clinician stories that are not specifically related to therapeutic issues. This client has also struggled to complete her homework assignments to engage in her physical therapy exercises following a recent injury. Although she remembers and knows how to do them the client reports that "she just can not find the motivation." Here the clinician could arrange the following contingency: If the client completes her exercises as assigned, she can spend 10 minutes of the following session discussing whatever she chooses. If the client fails to complete her exercises as assigned, no time will be left for off topic discussion and the clinician will spend time doing a functional assessment of why the assignment was not completed (experienced by many clients as mildly punishing). While the specific contingency here is arbitrary, this intervention takes advantage of the clinician as a reinforcer as recommended by FAP. More on how to use the therapeutic relationship to shape client behavior is covered in Point 28.

The BA clinician can also find creative ways to become involved in managing contingencies for client behavior, even when they do not have control over a powerful reinforcer. Consider a client who absolutely must complete a task before the following session, such as filing student loan paperwork. In this situation the clinician could attempt to manipulate contingencies by saying the following:

> It looks like you absolutely need to get this done. What if we tried something to give you a little more incentive? What if you wrote a check out right now to your least favorite political party? If you show up next week without doing your assignment, I will mail the check. If you do complete the assignment we can tear it up.

Here the clinician has added a punishment contingency to inactivity in order to increase the likelihood of activation. It is important to note that any contingency involving the clinician providing contingencies for out-of-session behavior is somewhat arbitrary and clearly temporary (e.g., the contingency ends when therapy ends). Thus it is imperative that the clinician not over-rely on these interventions as ultimately non-depressed client behavior only will be maintained by natural, real world contingencies. See Point 26 for more on this issue.

25

Mindful valued activation

Often the most important activation assignments lead to immediate increases in feelings of depression, anxiety or other discomfort. Other assignments elicit negative thoughts or painful memories. Getting out of bed in the morning is hard. Exercising requires continued effort in the presence of fatigue, aches, and cramps. Looking for a job, updating one's résumé, applying for jobs, and going on interviews all raise self-doubt, self-criticism, and thoughts of continued failure and rejection. These private consequences can be important factors in controlling inactivity and establishing strong competing contingencies against activity.

The primacy and role of such private consequences in psychopathology, broadly speaking, has been noted by several authors. Hayes and colleagues (Hayes, Wilson, Gifford, Follette, & Strosahl, 1996) labeled behaviors controlled by the avoidance of aversive private experiences *experiential avoidance*. They suggest that experiential avoidance represents a broad, functionally defined, psychopathological dimension that cuts across many diagnostic categories, and developed ACT procedures to target these problems. David Barlow and his colleagues (2004) similarly have suggested that preventing emotional avoidance is one of three fundamental therapeutic components necessary for the treatment of emotional (depression and anxiety) disorders. Likewise, the version of BA by Martell and colleagues (2001) primarily targeted such forms of avoidance with a variety of treatment techniques. We loosely label this set of techniques *mindful valued activation*, to highlight the roles that mindful awareness and values play when activating in the face of competing experiential contingencies.

Our discussion of this issue is largely consistent with Martell and colleagues (2001), with the suggestion that mindful valued activation occur only after functional assessment suggests that private consequences are a primary obstacle to activation and simple activation has failed. Although other interventions already described (stimulus control, skills training, and contingency management) may occur in tandem with simple activation, mindful valued activation represents a step up from simple activation in terms of complexity and difficulty (for both the client and clinician). In other words, mindful valued activation represents a change in how activation is to occur. Thus, because our goal throughout this book was to describe our simple, expedient, and efficient version of BA, we suggest that the techniques described below are used only when necessary.

Discussing avoidance with the client in BA

When discussing experiential avoidance with clients, we have found it helpful to use a "three circles" diagram (Figure 5) to provide an overall rationale, which is a modification of the work of Martell and colleagues (2001). Moving clockwise from the upper left, the first circle represents life events and the second circle represents depressive symptoms that are natural responses to these triggers. For example, a death of a spouse or loss of a job (negative life event) may function to elicit some of the symptoms of depression (e.g., crying, sadness, flat affect), as well as other affective responses (e.g., anxiety). When using the diagram, we recommend that the clinician and client first collaboratively list life events in the circle, which the clinician then labels *life events*, then they do the same for *symptoms*, with the clinician drawing an arrow from life events to symptoms to highlight the relationship. The clinician should highlight that the relationship between negative life events and depressive symptoms is natural, normal and occurs for all human beings. It is key to highlight to clients that these symptoms of depression and related symptoms make sense given the individual's

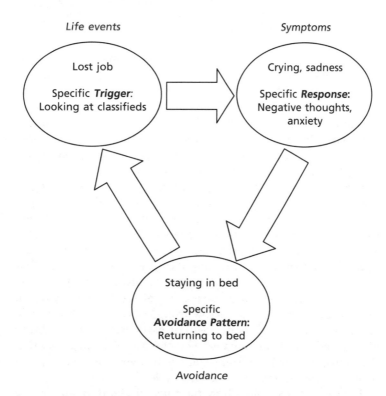

Figure 5 Explaining avoidance to clients with the "three circles" diagram

context—given the context the individual *should be* feeling the way he or she is feeling. Experiencing the symptoms of depression does not mean that one is crazy, it means that difficult negative life events have happened and the individual is reacting to them as humans do.

The BA clinician then asks the client to discuss how he or she has been *responding to these responses*. Specifically, the clinician highlights that when an individual experiences these aversive symptoms it is natural to want to avoid them in any way possible, and asks the client to think about the ways he or she may have been avoiding. Clients usually provide accurate responses here, including staying in bed, drinking alcohol or using drugs, avoiding going to work, avoiding picking up the phone, trying not to think about certain things, and so on. These responses often include some of the behavioral symptoms of depression such as over eating, hypersomnia, and staying in bed. The clinician may label these responses *avoidance* and draw an arrow to the avoidance circle from the symptoms circle to suggest the relationship between the two.

Clients generally can see where this discussion is leading at this point—although the avoidance response makes sense given the context, it actually is making the situation worse in the long run, contributing to additional negative life events. Specifically, avoidance may lead to decreases in aversive private experiences in the short term but in the long term the negative events that caused the problem initially are unresolved and additional negative events may accumulate as a result. The clinician demonstrates this with an arrow from avoidance to life events, suggesting that this response pattern may result in a spiral into deeper and deeper depression. The clinician then suggests that they must come up with alternatives to avoidance when faced with such symptoms to break this cycle.

Figure 5 also suggests how the three circles diagram can be used to illustrate specific instances of avoidance, using the acronym *TRAP* from Martell and colleagues (2001), with the *T* standing for *Trigger* (specific instance of a life event), the *R* standing for *Response* (specific instance of symptoms), and the *AP* standing for *Avoidance Pattern* (specific instance of avoidance). Consider Jim, who was assigned to look through the classifieds and identify three jobs that he could seek out the following week. Although he sat down at the scheduled time with the newspaper and began to look (the *trigger*), Jim reported that as soon as he began he was assaulted with negative thoughts (e.g., "Why am I even trying, I am never going to get a job") and physiological anxiety (e.g., chest tightening). These were his specific *responses*. Jim reported quickly ending his search and lying down in bed (the *avoidance pattern*). Furthermore, Jim reported that the negative thoughts and anxiety quickly subsided once he stopped looking, but he felt very inadequate for having gone another week without making any progress.

An initial task would be for Jim to identify this as a *TRAP* and to identify other *TRAPs* that are contributing to his depression. Identification of *TRAPs* is a simple way to increase client awareness of relevant elicited responses to difficult activation assignments and also serves as a prompt to engage in *Alternative Coping* behavior. In other words, we want Jim to "get out of the trap and get back on trac[k]" (*Trigger, Response, Alternate Coping*; Martell et al., 2001; p. 102); in this case mindfully approaching negative thoughts and anxiety by continuing engagement in job seeking in their presence, as we discuss next.

Mindfulness

Mindfulness interventions have been proposed by a variety of authors and in fact have become one of the defining features of a "third wave" of psychotherapy approaches that includes BA (Hayes et al., 2004). These third-wave authors typically strip the interventions of any spiritual connotations and focus on their core characteristics. For example, Dimidjian and Linehan (2003) define mindfulness as follows:

> Mindfulness is understood simply as awareness of what is, at the level of direct and immediate experience, separate from concepts, category, and expectations. It is a way of living awake, with your eyes wide open. Mindfulness as a practice is the act of repetitively directing your attention to only one thing. And that one thing is the one moment you are alive— allowing the moment, so to speak . . . Mindfulness is thus the practice of willingness to be alive to the moment and radical acceptance of the entirety of moment.
>
> (p. 229)

Linehan (1993) distinguishes the "what" of mindfulness from the "how" of mindfulness, and we find this distinction useful. Regarding "what," Linehan (p. 111) emphasizes a process of observation, or what may be thought of simply as focused attention, during which one notices the ongoing stream of one's experience without getting caught in that stream. What one becomes mindful of is free to vary, as long as it occurs in the present moment. For example, a simple mindfulness exercise may consist of focused attention on one's breath, paying attention to the rise and fall of one's chest and the feel and heat of the air as it enters and exits one's body. Alternately, one may become mindful of one's thoughts, noticing as they come and go, watching them coming and going *and* noticing how one can quickly get hooked by a thought and enter into it completely, losing mindful observation for a moment (i.e., engaging with the content of thinking).

Mindfulness may focus on any sensory experience. For example, one may focus on auditory sensations and become present to the subtle noises that are ever-present in the environment, such as the hum of the air conditioner, the distant rumble of traffic, and the *sound* of one's breathing. Likewise, one may become mindful of a multi-sensory experience, such as the full experience of eating a chocolate chip cookie—the tastes and textures and how they change over time.

Regarding "how," Linehan (1993) notes that mindfulness is non-judgmental—any experience, no matter how potentially aversive, may be approached mindfully and without judgment. A cancer patient may practice mindfulness with respect to the pain of a tumor. An amputee may mindfully approach the pain of a phantom limb. A panic sufferer may be mindful of a rapidly beating heart. A person with generalized anxiety disorder may be mindful of the steady stream of idiosyncratic worries that fills her mind. A firefighter may mindfully experience fear as he enters a burning building and a soldier as he approaches a battlefield. Such mindfulness is a behavioral skill and takes practice like any behavior. Buddhist monks practice for years to achieve states of mindfulness that most of us will never achieve, allowing for extreme acts of non-judgmental acceptance of aversive experience, such as the famous burning protests during the Vietnam War.

For the purposes of BA, mindfulness can be framed as any simple assignment to focus attention or remain aware of the present moment when experiencing aversive private experiences, such as depressive rumination, that limit activation. For many clients, additional interventions will be required. As a starter, we recommend the brief guidelines provided by Dimidjian and Linehan (2003) that include didactic instruction, in-session practice, and corrective feedback, but we note that the more involved mindfulness procedures of ACT and DBT are consonant with BA. These approaches offer multiple clever, in-session and out-of-session exercises that promote and shape mindfulness and we recommend that clinicians learn these more advanced techniques for use with complicated or treatment refractory clients.

In general, the important point for the BA clinician is that the goal is to alter the manner in which the client responds to his or her own thoughts, feelings, and other bodily sensations that evoke avoidance. By mindfully attending to these stimuli, the avoidance evoking properties of the stimuli may in fact weaken, allowing for alternate approach behavior to occur. This paradox—that mindful acceptance of private experience reduces the salience of that private experience—actually has garnered considerable empirical support (e.g., Cioffi & Holloway, 1993; Masedo & Esteve, 2007; Wegner & Zanakos, 1994).

Incorporating values into mindful activation

In addition to being fundamental to the creation of BA activity hierarchies, values have an additional role to play with regards to mindful experiential approach. Again consider Jim. Jim is faced with the task of repeatedly approaching the aversive task of looking for jobs, despite the fact that it may take several months for the task to produce the desired consequence. In addition to working with Jim on allowing himself to mindfully experience the negative thoughts and anxiety that naturally occurred in response to looking at the classifieds, Jim's clinician asked Jim to revisit his values assessment and discussed with him how strongly he indeed valued meaningful employment. How can Jim's values become sufficiently salient to him, such that they sustain behavior in the face of continued, immediately aversive consequences?

Consider Vic, an overweight, depressed middle aged man with chronic back pain. His doctors have told him that he needs to lose weight and exercise more, and that if he does, over time his back pain may reduce. The time frame involved, however, is very long term, as it may take Vic years of effort to meaningfully impact his back pain. In addition, the immediate consequences of attempts at reduced caloric intake and increased exercise are quite aversive—increased hunger, increased pain and sore muscles—strongly favoring inactivity.

Ultimately, once Jim and Vic have identified their values, incorporating those values to evoke and sustain behavior is an issue of stimulus control. Specifically, Jim and Vic need specific cues in their environments to trigger value-driven behavior— perhaps a note on the bathroom mirror stating, "Remember what is important," pictures of their children or grandchildren in their wallets, or something else that they feel will serve as personal and meaningful reminders. Some clients have found it helpful to schedule personal time in the mornings such as a walk to provide an opportunity to reflect on the day and focus on values. The goal is for Jim and Vic to wake up each morning and re-commit to valued behavior, knowing full well that the day may be aversive. At the end of each day, we want Jim and Vic in essence to reflect on their days and say to themselves, "My problems remain, but today was a good day." The next morning, we want them to do the same thing over again.

Mindful valued activation in the therapy relationship

Because the stimuli that evoke experiential avoidance are the private experiences of the client, the client potentially brings these stimuli with him or her into the therapy room. This is quite important because, as stated above, mindfulness is a skill that can be shaped much more quickly through live practice and feedback than through simple instruction. Thus, clinician observation of client experiential avoidance during the therapy hour presents important opportunities to shape mindful valued activation (Tsai et al., 2008). For clients with problems related to experiential avoidance, the goal is mindful contact with the very experiences they want to avoid. This is akin to interoceptive exposure as per treatment for Panic Disorder (Barlow, 2002), but while interoceptive exposure is designed to *reduce* panic sensations, in-session mindfulness is designed to *facilitate* valued activation.

The question, "What are you feeling right now?" may be enough to trigger such in-session work. For a client who responds that they are experiencing, or trying not to experience, an unwanted emotion, a mindfulness therapeutic intervention may be:

> I see that you are struggling with your emotions at this point. I'd like to ask you to gently move into the experience rather than fighting it and, without judgment, tell me what you are feeling. Where do you feel it? In your chest? Behind your eyes? In your shoulders? Take your time with this and mindfully explore this feeling for me if you are able. I will be here for you and I am open to anything you may experience.

The BA clinician also may want to explore how the client's focus on trying not to feel something in session affects the therapy session and the therapy relationship. The clinician may highlight that trying not to feel results in distance between them and makes it harder for the clinician to understand the client. In contrast, if the client successfully engages in mindful awareness and expression of the unwanted emotion, the clinician may want to provide feedback to the client that such contact improves the therapy hour, makes it more meaningful, and makes the clinician feel closer to the client (of course, all this must be genuinely felt by the clinician). The ultimate goal is for the therapy hour to be a setting where the client can practice being mindful and focused on valued action, to make the most of the therapy hour and therapy relationship, as a training ground for other valued relationships.

26

Ending therapy

BA offers a distinct stance on termination. Specifically, from a BA perspective, the therapy and therapeutic relationship are relevant features of the client's environment that have changed since the beginning of treatment, and this support inevitably will be withdrawn when treatment is terminated. The nature and timing of termination and the relapse prevention measures employed in BA must reflect that therapy is a non-permanent and artificial environmental feature.

It is easy to imagine how attending therapy and engaging in a therapeutic relationship can support non-depressed behavior. Both aversive consequences for depressed behavior (e.g., monetary fines for missing a session, letting the clinician down by being inactive) and positive reinforcement for non-depressed behavior (e.g., clinician supportive statements, "feeling heard" by the clinician) are provided by the clinician over the course of therapy. Furthermore, especially for clients who are very isolated and inactive, the therapy situation provides salient prompts for non-depressed behaviors, such as getting dressed, leaving the house, having a conversation, and engaging in activation assignments. Clients may work extremely hard to please their clinicians and it is important to consider the clinician's role as a provider of clinically relevant consequences.

Thus, even if BA accomplishes its goal of activating new non-depressed behaviors, it is possible that these behaviors are not yet maintained by natural reinforcement in the outside environment and are under the control of therapy-related contingencies. Thus, transitioning control of non-depressed behaviors from arbitrary, therapy-related reinforcers to natural reinforcers available in the client's daily life should be a focus of

BA as termination approaches. A primary strategy implemented in BA is to increase the time between sessions as a way to fade from the arbitrary weekly session schedule to a no-therapy schedule. For example, a clinician could move from weekly sessions to bi-weekly sessions, to bi-weekly phone sessions, and to occasional informal phone check-ins.

Another implication of BA's contextual philosophy is that the environment the client is living in at the end of treatment will inevitably change. Eventually life events will occur that rob the client of sources of positive reinforcement. Thus, as treatment ends, BA clinicians seek to pair environmental change with the provision of skills to respond more effectively to future shifts in reinforcement contingencies, negative life events, and major life changes. These skills may be quite different from the skills targeted by skills training which focus on repertoire building. These skills focus on awareness of one's environment, self-assessment, and self-activation.

For example, the client can be provided with a *Staying Active Guide*. In our work at the University of Wisconsin-Milwaukee, this guide has included simple lists of (1) ways the client will recognize if they are becoming depressed or inactive again (to evoke self-activation as early as possible), (2) activities that the client enjoys when not depressed (to provide reminders of simple activation targets), (3) activities that are in line with the clients values that they may not feel like doing, (4) obstacles to engaging in #2 and #3 and plans for overcoming those obstacles, and (5) expected future events that may be difficult for the client to handle (holidays, anniversaries, changes of seasons, or specific things the client's partner may do or may not do), and plans for responding to these events. These lists or others tailored to the client can be collaboratively developed with the client over the last several sessions and given to the client to take home for future reference. The guide also may include the clinician's or clinic's phone number and the invitation to restart therapy or have booster sessions if things get rough.

We end this Point with two brief examples for how this guide can be employed. Maria was worried that in September, when her children would be going back to school, the increased isolation and lack of direction would be depressing for her. She and her clinician discussed ways she could proactively address this situation, such as volunteering at her children's school during the day. In addition, as most of the enjoyable activities Maria engaged in at the time of termination involved her children (e.g., organizing play dates with other families, watching tee-ball games), a list of potentially enjoyable activities not involving her children was generated (e.g., going to coffee with friends, scheduling time to paint).

When discussing termination with his clinician, Jeff was aware that his company would be downsizing soon and that he may lose his job. Jeff and his clinician identified this as a potential future event that would likely affect his mood. Jeff wrote on his guide that he would immediately engage in active job seeking, and he and his clinician developed a list of active job-seeking behaviors (e.g., updating his résumé, checking the classifieds) to guide this self-activation. Potential obstacles to these activities (e.g., "Looking for a job will bring up thoughts about how unfair it was that I lost my last job") were discussed and problem solved. In addition, Jeff and his clinician collaboratively came up with a list of possible places to search for employment to aid in self-activation when and if Jeff lost his job. It was specifically noted that Jeff could recognize himself becoming depressed again if he started watching more TV and stopped cooking his meals. Jeff agreed to call his clinician for guidance if he noticed himself becoming depressed and his attempts at self-activation failed.

27

Thinking functionally about suicide and medication

Managing suicide in BA

Guidelines for suicide assessment and intervention that are consistent with BA may be found in several places (Bongar, 2002; Linehan, 1993). In general, suicide assessment and intervention requires a very active, problem-focused, and concrete analysis of the crisis situation, so a basic BA foundation should be helpful in focusing the clinician on what is required. As discussed in Martell et al. (2001), suicidal behavior is a problem behavior and the goal is to activate alternate behavior. Thus, standard activation procedures as discussed in this book apply, as long as the clinician is employing them in a way that is consistent with the standards of care for suicidal behavior (Bongar, 2002).

As discussed by Linehan (1993), we encourage the clinician to think functionally when weighing a decision to hospitalize or not to hospitalize. Specifically, as discussed in Point 4, the respondent and operant functions of suicidal crises should be considered. For acutely suicidal clients who do not have a history of suicidal crises, it may be that the suicidal crisis is precipitated by an overwhelming aversive respondent reaction that the client simply does not know how to problem solve. In such cases, temporary hospitalization to allow the client time to re-regulate his or her emotions and develop solutions may be indicated.

For chronically suicidal clients who have had repeated hospitalizations, however, additional hospitalization may serve an operant function, and the suicidal behavior may be partially maintained by the consequence of hospitalization, as it results in escape from responsibility, increased sympathy and concern, and so on. For these clients, it may be clinically indicated to take a calculated risk by not hospitalizing, conceptualize the behavior as avoidance, and implement avoidance activation procedures. For these clients, the clinician must learn to tolerate a certain level of chronic suicidal ideation. We recommend the procedures of DBT for such clients (Linehan, 1993).

Medication and BA

Research is clear that medications are helpful in the treatment of depression and it is becoming increasingly clear that the combination of medication and empirically supported psychotherapy for depression produces the best outcomes in terms of the total number of individuals treated to remission (Hollon et al., 2005). At the same time, it is clear to us that anti-depressant medications are overprescribed and many cases of depression can be successfully treated by BA without the use of anti-depressant medication.

The questions, then, are when to suggest medication to a BA client and what to do with a client who starts a course of BA already on medication? As always, we encourage the clinician to think functionally. First, when medications work, they seem to actually work faster on average than psychotherapy. Thus, medications that are activating may be useful early in therapy to jumpstart the activation process for clients who are particularly inactive. As discussed by Martell et al. (2001) and Leventhal and Martell (2006), with these clients the clinician should provide the rationale that medications may assist in the activation and problem solving processes. The clinician may suggest that, of course, medications affect the brain, but the focus of therapy should be on activation and improving the client's life and not on waiting for medications to "kick in" before activation can occur.

As the client improves it is important that the clinician shape the client's attributions about positive changes such that they are attributed to the client's hard work and not to the medication. Finally, as activation takes hold, the clinician should encourage the client to work with his or her pharmacotherapist to withdraw the medication over time. A typical pharmacotherapist may be reluctant to do this, so the clinician may choose to talk directly with the pharmacotherapist about this issue. We recommend that the clinician fortifies him or herself with data on this issue summarized succinctly in Hollon et al. (2005).

Second, for many clients, taking medication functions as an experiential avoidance behavior, in that the explicit purpose of taking medication is to quickly, immediately reduce aversive symptoms (see Hayes et al., 1996 for a relevant discussion of drug abuse as experiential avoidance). Taking medications is relatively easy and does not require much activation. For these clients, taking medication is indeed antithetical to BA to the extent that it blocks activation. These clients may be very scared to stop or even reduce their medication, and it is our experience that attempts to convince these clients to do so are generally unsuccessful. Instead, the clinician more likely will benefit from ignoring the specific medication issue as much as possible and focusing instead on experiential avoidance broadly, while looking for naturally occurring opportunities to help the client identify taking medications as a form of avoidance.

Finally, a BA clinician's functional stance against medication should not preclude him or her from referring a client to a pharmacotherapist if BA is not working, as medications do represent the standard of care. As research continues to accumulate, however, and the problematic, aggressive marketing practices of the pharmaceutical industry increasingly come to light (Angell, 2004; Valenstein, 1988), we do hope that standards of care will evolve to more accurately represent the value of behavioral approaches to depression treatment, and the problems with anti-depressant use, and we encourage BA clinicians to act as advocates and work toward making such public policy changes happen. In the meanwhile, however, working within our current standards of care is required to be an ethical practicing clinician, regardless of one's theoretical or personal views.

28

The therapeutic relationship in BA

The single most important behavioral process in BA is reinforcement. BA's focus on reinforcement establishes it as a member of a long line of successful behavioral treatments that have employed reinforcement to change behavior in controlled settings. In general, these procedures identify the target variable *as it occurs* live and apply reinforcement contingent on the occurrence of the target variable. A fundamental principle of these applied interventions is that if the clinician has direct access to these contingencies and can manipulate them directly, treatment should be more efficient and more effective.

Although BA focuses on reinforcement in the client's environment, many of the techniques employed by the clinician in the therapy room do not. Instead, a typical BA session consists of talk about the client's outside life and the clinician provides instruction, guidance, and coaching to the client on how to change his or her behavior outside of the session. The BA clinician certainly provides validation and empathy, expresses caring and concern, and exhibits patience and understanding, and these responses may be seen as reinforcing the very behavior of coming to therapy. These non-specific clinician reinforcing responses generally are seen as facilitating, but separate from the mechanism of action of BA.

This does not have to be the case. As we have discussed at length elsewhere (Busch, Manos, Rusch, Bowe, & Kanter, in press; Kanter, Manos, Busch, & Rusch, 2008) and throughout this book, many BA procedures may be conducted live in the therapy session and incorporate reinforcement procedures. Thus, the BA clinician can apply behavioral theory directly to client in-session behavior by applying techniques of FAP, which were developed specifically to augment treatments such as BA. Here we provide additional general information about doing this to supplement the material in earlier Points.

Identifying BA targets in the therapy relationship

BA targets often occur in the therapy relationship. Clients who have problems with establishing routines in their daily life often display inconsistent attendance and homework completion, change meeting times, show up late to session, and do not write future sessions in an appointment book. Clients with outside problems related to avoidance may avoid difficult topics in session or begin to show some emotion but then make a joke or change the topic. Passive clients may agree with all of the clinician's suggestions and advice, but demonstrate no real enthusiasm or follow-through.

BA clinicians should be on the lookout for such problems to occur in the therapy relationship for at least two reasons. First, clinician awareness of BA targets during the session provides the clinician with first hand access to the variables relevant to a functional assessment of the client's behavior. This is the outpatient clinician's only opportunity to observe client behavior directly and careful observation should lead to hypotheses regarding what the client's behavior actually looks like outside of session. For example, a clinician may notice that Bill shuts down in session and becomes quite passive following the slightest negative feedback from the clinician (e.g., the clinician expressing frustration that he was late for session). Here the clinician could ask:

We have been trying to figure out the important factors contributing to why you don't speak up as much as you would like with your wife. In this session, I noticed that you stopped talking after we discussed your being late for session. Does something similar happen with her, where you get some kind of negative feedback and kind of shut down?

Through these kind of questions the clinician may be able to create a more accurate case conceptualization for Bill that would identify negative interpersonal feedback as the antecedent to passive avoidance behavior.

Second, awareness of problem behaviors occurring in session provides a setting for the assignment of anti-depressant activities that are in line with BA treatment goals. Occurrences of live problem behaviors are prime opportunities to gently prompt the client and achieve activation *in the moment*, rather than simply talking about activation that hopefully will occur later. For example, a passive client can be prompted to take more control of the therapy session and an avoidant client can be prompted to stay on a difficult topic. In this way, the therapy relationship becomes a naturally occurring laboratory for practicing and developing alternative activation behaviors.

For example, an activation behavior for Bill may be to continue a conversation despite feeling slighted. Here the clinician may suggest:

> For the rest of session I would like to ask you to continue to engage with me even when some tough feelings come up.

The same BA considerations for daily life assignments can be helpful here. Specifically, the difficulty of the assignment should be graded and barriers to completion should be discussed and problem-solved.

Reinforcing BA targets in the therapy relationship

The key to BA is not just prompting non-depressed behaviors but that they are reinforced by the natural environment in such a way that the behavior is strengthened and maintained over time. When BA targets occur in session, the clinician becomes a purveyor of such reinforcement. The key to reinforcing BA targets as they occur in the therapy relationship is recognizing that the best way to be reinforcing is to be as natural as possible, such that the nature of the reinforcement that occurs in session will be similar to what is hoped to occur outside of session. Some attempts to reinforce, such as saying "good job" or providing praise in some other way, are not natural and for that reason are discouraged as responses to in-session behaviors.

What is naturally reinforcing? This of course will vary depending on the target. Assertiveness is naturally reinforced by compliance with an assertive request. This can be deceptively tricky. For example, responding to an unassertive client who asks for the window to be opened is easy—open the window. Responding to that same client when he asks for extra therapy time may be more difficult. In general, the goal is to give the client what he or she wants, within the confines of the boundaries of a curative and ethical therapeutic relationship.

Often, the kinds of client problems that show up in the therapy relationship involve interpersonal avoidance. In these cases, displays of vulnerability and emotional disclosure in session may be seen as activation targets that would be reinforced by increased intimacy and connection in the therapy relationship. Thus, the best clinician reinforcing responses often include amplification of private reactions, including showing caring, telling the client how the clinician feels about him/her in the moment, and non-verbal displays of interpersonal connection.

Again consider Bill. After being given the assignment, Bill effectively engaged the clinician in an honest discussion about how he felt when the clinician criticized him. The clinician recognized this as an improvement for Bill:

I truly am sorry for being insensitive to you here. I also have to note how helpful it is for me to hear from you directly that you were hurt. When you are open with me, it helps me understand you better and makes you more human to me. How do you think your wife would respond if you were more open to her as well?

Notice how the clinician completed the parallel with Bill's wife and suggested an activation assignment in which the behavior Bill successfully completed in session is now taken "on the road" and tried with his wife. When this occurs in BA, the therapy relationship may become a vehicle for meaningful interpersonal change that would be difficult to achieve without a focus on the therapy relationship, and the bounds of what is possible in BA are expanded greatly.

When to focus on the therapy relationship?

We believe that the focus on the therapy relationship as discussed here should make BA more effective, and more meaningful, for many clients. The focus, however, may be particularly useful for clients with comorbid depression and personality disorders, and for clients whose depressive presentations are characterized by interpersonal problems generally. It may also be useful for depression in the context of marital distress, particularly when the non-depressed member of the couple can not or will not participate in the therapy process. We note, however, that although the use of the therapy relationship in BA as discussed here is theoretically consistent and research suggests that FAP techniques can improve CT (Kohlenberg, Kanter, Bolling, Parker, & Tsai, 2002), future research is required to provide empirical support for the specific integration of FAP and BA techniques.

29

A distinct flexible framework: Adaptations for minorities

We believe that BA's focus on contextual determinants of depression may be a particularly good fit for ethnic minorities, for whom depression is often characterized by seemingly overwhelming environmental hardships. For example, consider the following list of problems related to depression that may be experienced by low-income ethnic minorities:

- difficulties with obtaining, maintaining, and upward mobility in employment, or being paid a wage that makes it impossible to pay bills or escape from poverty;
- health problems including obesity, physical pain from injuries, and chronic health conditions;
- daily hassles that are increased exponentially when living in economic distress such as use of public transportation, car maintenance, finding quality daycare if employed, and lack of insurance;
- problems stemming from not being able to speak English such as not fully understanding contracts or bills, difficulty negotiating agencies and businesses;
- direct and indirect experiences of racism and discrimination.

It may be that BA techniques emphasizing perseverance, action and empowerment in the face of these hardships may both be more acceptable to ethnic minorities and ultimately more efficacious than techniques that locate the problem of depression within the individual (e.g., cognitive or biological factors). However, adaptations to increase the cultural sensitivity of BA also are necessary. Here we explicitly outline why and how BA may be adapted for Latinos and African Americans in the United

States, but these issues may be applied equally to other ethnic minorities and to the minority experience in other countries.

Depressed Latinos

Recently Santiago-Rivera and colleagues (in press) presented a culturally and linguistically adapted version of BA for depressed Latinos, primarily adapting the Martell and colleagues (2001) version of BA. Several adaptations to BA were made. First, emphasis was placed on free, low-cost, and culturally sensitive sources of positive reinforcement. For example, simple activation assignments included:

- dancing
- walking (outside or in a mall in Winter)
- community center activities and groups, such as relaxation and stress management groups
- borrowing fitness DVDs from library
- going to a museum (often museums have free days once a week)
- attending seasonal free concerts (in the park or at the mall)
- visiting friends
- going to church, and various church activities and events
- calling one's family in one's country of origin (this is not free but clients can be activated to make sure their calling plan is good and rates can be very inexpensive)
- playing with children
- gardening
- listening to music
- window shopping
- cooking
- cleaning house
- knitting.

Second, adaptations to the first session were made to increase treatment retention. Because acculturation is often a factor, many Latino clients may lack knowledge of the psychotherapy process and maintain strong cultural ties and values associated with their ethnic origins. Thus the first session consisted of a relatively structured culturally sensitive review of the psychotherapy process in general and BA in particular. The first session also involved provision of the treatment rationale, discussion of medication, discussion of potential family involvement in therapy, and provision of an initial activation homework assignment.

Finally, Latino-specific values and beliefs also were important to assess and incorporate into treatment, including *familismo* (valuing of close connections and relationships with one's family), *personalismo* (valuing of relationships in general and responsiveness to the personal dimension of relationships), *marianismo* (women are to be self-sacrificing toward their families and children, pure, long-suffering, nurturing and pious), and *machismo* (men are to provide for, protect, and defend the family, and are to be honorable and respected for having this responsibility; Santiago-Rivera, Arredondo, & Gallardo-Cooper, 2002). Notice that together these values tend to center on the importance of family and maintaining a particular hierarchical structure within the family with authority given to husbands and fathers. Simply put, the important issue for BA was that depression should be understood in the context of these values, and activation assignments should be sensitive to and not contradict them (unless doing so is in line with the client's goals).

Depressed African Americans

Similar to Latinos, there are salient contextual risk factors for depression in African Americans. These contextual risk factors include low socioeconomic status (Riolo et al., 2005), decreased social support (Kimbrough, Molock, & Walton, 1996; Lincoln, Chatters, & Taylor, 2005), poor health (Jonas & Mussolino, 2000; Miller et al., 2004), and experiences of racism (Clark, Anderson, Clark, & Williams, 1999; Fernando, 1984). Although less work has occurred modifying BA for African Americans, we suggest that BA may be a good fit for African American depression as well, as it directly targets these contextual risk factors with a structured system of activation and empowerment.

In addition, BA may be a good fit in terms of the unique clinical presentation of African Americans with depression. Specifically, African Americans compared to Caucasians experience increased somatic symptoms related to sleeping and eating patterns (Brown, Schulberg, & Madonia, 1996) which may be directly targeted by BA. In addition, religious faith is very important to many African Americans, and depression may coincide with a decrease in faith related activities. Thus, activation assignments may directly target this by encouraging reengagement with the church and discussions with pastors or other religious leaders.

In fact, many African Americans seek the church rather than mental health specialists for help with mental health problems. Thus, it is important to consider how BA strategies and techniques are consistent with religious and pastoral recommendations. To the extent that a pastor recommends to a depressed individual that he or she should pray and have faith in God for help, and offers no other recommendations, BA is not consistent with such guidance. However, to the extent that, in addition to encouraging prayer and faith, the pastor also recommends that the individual seeks out social support, tries to reconnect with family, becomes more active and engaged at work, and so forth, BA is quite consistent. Thus, an interesting avenue for future research to explore would be to work with the African American faith community to see if pastoral counseling can be improved with BA strategies.

General considerations

It may be worthwhile to note one tricky aspect of activation with ethnic or other minorities. Specifically, sensitivity is needed in determining if a specific activation is actually feasible. For example, consider a Latina who is not a citizen and is working for a racist boss. It may be very detrimental to suggest an activation assignment that she confront her boss about his racism. If the desirable activation of confronting the specific individual is not feasible, what alternate activation can be suggested? In general, we emphasize and validate the experience of righteous anger in our clients and empowerment and political action can be used as general activation strategies rather than confronting specific individuals.

It is our hope that BA may be broadly applicable to Latinos, African Americans and other ethnic and sexual minorities. We believe the basic BA framework is easily adaptable to different cultural groups, with close collaboration and consultation with members of these groups to ensure culturally sensitive treatment. BA focuses on contextual factors in depression which, compared to intrapsychic factors emphasized by some other treatments, may be less likely to be imbued with culturally specific meanings and thus more easily adapted to different cultures. Ultimately, the BA model may be a useful cross-cultural model because it contains very few culturally specific assumptions and allows for individual assessment and values to determine the activation targets. Broadly speaking, to the extent that these groups have higher rates of depression because of significant environmental hardships, BA may offer a compelling fit.

30

The promise of BA

We believe that BA offers great promise as a simple, pragmatic treatment for depression. A BA clinician does not need to be steeped in behavioral theory but does need to appreciate the basics of functional contextualism and a broad definition of reinforcement and behavior. Most importantly, the BA clinician needs to be able to think about and conceptualize client problems functionally. With this understanding in place, the model and treatment of depression are relatively simple. In this book, we have tried to clarify this model and re-organize the existing BA techniques into a straight-forward structure that minimizes the need for advanced training and maximizes the power and efficiency of BA. It does this through a stepped-care approach that starts with simple activation and proceeds to more complex, individualized techniques only as necessary. In this way, this approach streamlines the therapeutic hour for each client and allows the clinician to allocate clinical time and resources to those clients who need it most. At the same time, the therapeutic experience of the client is rich, focused on values, purpose and meaning, and the therapeutic relationship may be intimate and intense, regardless of whether the treatment is brief or prolonged.

In sum, the simplicity of the approach highlights BA's strength as an easy-to-train and thus widely disseminable approach, and the efficiency of the approach may be especially important in today's managed care environment. A clinician in such an environment easily can add BA techniques into his or her current repertoire without much disruption. At the same time, the model may be elaborated for more complex presentations, including personality disorders, and it may be adapted relatively easily for culturally diverse clients. Although we currently are in the process of evaluating this specific approach to BA, as we have noted throughout this book, the basic techniques of BA, both individually and in various combinations, have a wealth of empirical support to their credit.

Broadly speaking, BA offers a set of techniques for empowering the individual to change the environment to support healthy behavior, leading to sustained, valued activation and a life of meaning and purpose. This focus on context and positive contextual change is not unique to BA, as BA shares this vision with several other *third-wave* psychotherapies, notably ACT. With this in mind, we also are optimistic that the BA model and techniques, like those of ACT, may be applicable for a variety of disorders in addition to depression, functionally linked to BA by the common theme that the current and historical contexts have created problematic behavioral repertoires that are changeable through BA's *outside-in* approach.

A final promise of BA is its potential to change attitudes about what depression is at a fundamental level. BA asserts that depression is best conceptualized not as a disease but rather in terms of the context of clients' lives. Simply put, it is not a client's fault that he or she became depressed. It is not a product of being lazy, unmotivated, or unable to pull one's self up by one's bootstraps. The client does not want to be depressed and in fact is responding to his or her environment in understandable and predictable ways. Furthermore, although biological changes occur in depression, depression is not a product of a biochemical imbalance, something wrong with one's brain, or faulty genetics. Depression makes sense given one's history and one's current environment. In this way, the BA model is very non-blaming and potentially de-stigmatizing for a condition that, after all, many people prefer not to disclose to others or even admit to themselves. Most importantly, it is a condition for which many do not seek treatment and the behavioral model may lead to increased treatment seeking (Rusch et al., in press). This view that depression is a function of context also generates great empathy, but it is an active empathy, focused on empowering individuals to change their lives and make the world a better, less depressing place. This holds for BA clinicians as much as it does for BA clients.

This social message is not unique to BA and in fact dates back to the original writings of B. F. Skinner (e.g., 1953), who provided the initial provocative seeds that grew into modern behavioral theory. Skinner's goal, from the beginning, was constructive, positive social change, and his development of the philosophy of radical behaviorism was an explicit attempt to design a philosophy of science that would lead to productive clinical and scientific efforts to achieve such change. BA is part of this lineage and this social effort. We hope that the clarifications, unifications, and distinctions offered by the current book result in a small, but meaningful, contribution.

References

Addis, M. E., & Carpenter. K. M. (1999). Why, why, why?: Reason-giving and rumination as predictors of response activation and insight-oriented treatment rationales. *Journal of Clinical Psychology*, *55*, 881–894.

Angell, M. (2004). *The truth about the drug companies: How they deceive us and what to do about it*. New York: Crown Publishing Group.

Barlow, D. (2002). *Anxiety and its disorders: The nature and treatment of anxiety and panic* (2nd ed.). New York: Guilford Press.

Barlow, D. H., Allen, L. B., & Choate, M. L. (2004). Toward a unified treatment for emotional disorders. *Behavior Therapy*, *35*, 205–230.

Beck, A. T., Rush, A. J., Shaw, B. F., & Emery, G. (1979). *Cognitive therapy of depression*. New York: Guilford.

Beck, A. T., Steer, R. A., & Brown, G. K. (1996). *Manual for Beck Depression Inventory-II*. San Antonio, TX: Psychological Corporation.

Bongar, B. (2002). *The suicidal patient: Clinical and legal standards of care* (2nd ed.). Washington, DC: American Psychological Association.

Brown, C., Schulberg, H., & Madonia, M. (1996). Clinical presentations of major depression by African Americans and whites in primary medical care practice. *Journal of Affective Disorders*, *41*, 181–191.

Busch, A. M., Kanter, J. W., Landes, S. J., & Kohlenberg, R. J. (2006).

Sudden gains and outcome: A broader temporal analysis of cognitive therapy for depression. *Behavior Therapy, 37*, 61–68.

Busch, A. M., Manos, R. C., Rusch, L. C., Bowe, W. M., & Kanter, J. W. (in press). FAP and behavioral activation. In J. W. Kanter, M. Tsai, & R. J. Kohlenberg (Eds.), *Functional analytic psychotherapy in practice*. New York: Springer.

Cioffi, D., & Holloway, J. (1993). Delayed costs of suppressed pain. *Journal of Personality and Social Psychology, 64*, 274–282.

Clark, R., Anderson, N. B., Clark, V. R., & Williams, D. R. (1999). Racism as a stressor for African Americans. *American Psychologist, 54*, 805–816.

Cuijpers, P., van Straten, A., & Warmerdam, L. (2007). Behavioral activation treatments of depression: A meta-analysis. *Clinical Psychology Review, 27*, 318–326.

Dimidjian, S., Hollon, S. D., Dobson, K. S., Schmaling, K. B., Kohlenberg, R. J., Addis, M. E., et al. (2006). Randomized trial of behavioral activation, cognitive therapy, and antidepressant medication in the acute treatment of adults with major depression. *Journal of Consulting and Clinical Psychology, 74*, 658–670.

Dimidjian, S., & Linehan, M. (2003) Mindfulness practice. In W. O'Donohue, J. E. Fisher, & S. C. Hayes (Eds.), *Cognitive behavior therapy: Applying empirically supported techniques in your practice*. Hoboken, NJ: John Wiley & Sons, Inc.

Dobson, K. S., Hollon, S. D., Dimidjian, S. A., Schmaling, K. B., Kohlenberg, R. J., Rizvi, S., et al. (2004, May). Prevention of relapse. In S. D. Hollon (Chair), *Behavioral activation, cognitive therapy, and antidepressant medication in the treatment of major depression*. Symposium presented at the annual meeting of the American Psychiatric Association, New York, NY.

Ellis, A. (1962). *Reason and emotion in psychotherapy*. Secaucus, NJ: Citadel.

Fernando, S. (1984). Racism as a cause of depression. *The International Journal of Social Psychiatry, 30*, 41–49.

Ferster, C. (1973). A functional analysis of depression. *American Psychologist, 28*, 857–870.

Foa, E., Hembree, E., & Rothbaum, B. (2007). *Prolonged exposure therapy for PTSD: Emotional processing of traumatic experiences: Therapist guide*. New York: Oxford University Press.

Franklin, M., & Foa, E. (2008). Obsessive-compulsive disorder. In D. H. Barlow (Ed.), *Clinical handbook of psychological disorders: A step-by-step treatment manual* (4th ed.). New York: Guilford Press.

Gaynor, S. T., & Harris, A. (2008). Single-participant assessment of treatment mediators: Strategy description and examples from a behavioral activation intervention for depressed adolescents. *Behavior Modification, 32*, 372–402.

Gifford, E., & Hayes, S. (1999). Functional contextualism: A pragmatic philosophy for behavioral science. In W. O'Donohue & R. Kitchener (Eds.), *Handbook of behaviorism*. San Diego, CA: Academic Press.

Gortner, E. T., Gollan, J. K., Dobson, K. S., & Jacobson, N. S. (1998). Cognitive-behavioral treatment for depression: Relapse prevention. *Journal of Consulting and Clinical Psychology, 66*, 377–384.

Hayes, S. C. (1993). Analytic goals and the varieties of scientific contextualism. In S. C. Hayes, L. J. Hayes, H. W. Reese, & T. R. Sarbin (Eds.), *Varieties of scientific contextualism*. Reno, NV: Context Press.

Hayes, S. C., Barnes-Holmes, D., & Roche, B. (2001). *Relational frame theory: A post-Skinnerian account of human language and cognition*. New York: Kluwer Academic/Plenum Publishers.

Hayes, S. C., & Brownstein, A. (1986). Mentalism, behavior-behavior relations, and a behavior-analytic view of the purposes of science. *Behavior Analyst, 9*, 175–190.

Hayes, S. C., Follette, V., & Linehan, M. (2004). *Mindfulness and acceptance: Expanding the cognitive-behavioral tradition*. New York: Guilford Press.

Hayes, S. C., Hayes, L. J., Reese, H. W., & Sarbin, T. R. (Eds.) (1988). *Varieties of scientific contextualism*. Reno, NV: Context Press.

Hayes, S. C., Luoma, J., Bond, F., Masuda, A., & Lillis, J. (2006). Acceptance and commitment therapy: Model, processes and outcomes. *Behaviour Research and Therapy, 44*, 1–25.

Hayes, S. C., Strosahl, K., & Wilson, K. (1999). *Acceptance and commitment therapy: An experiential approach to behavior change*. New York: Guilford Press.

Hayes, S. C., Wilson, K., Gifford, E., Follette, V., & Strosahl, K. (1996). Experiential avoidance and behavioral disorders: A functional dimensional approach to diagnosis and treatment. *Journal of Consulting and Clinical Psychology, 64*, 1152–1168.

Heidt, J. M., & Marx, B. P. (2003). Self-monitoring as a treatment vehicle. In W. O'Donohue, J. E. Fisher, & S. C. Hayes (Eds.), *Cognitive behavior therapy: Applying empirically supported techniques in your practice*. Hoboken, NJ: John Wiley & Sons, Inc.

Herrnstein, R. J. (1970). On the law of effect. *Journal of the Experimental Analysis of Behavior, 13*, 243–266.

Hollon, S. D., Jarrett, R., Nierenberg, A., Thase, M., Trivedi, M., & Rush, A. (2005). Psychotherapy and medication in the treatment of adult and geriatric depression: Which monotherapy or combined treatment? *Journal of Clinical Psychiatry*, *66*, 455–468.

Hopko, D. R., Lejuez, C. W., LePage, J. P., Hopko, S. D., & McNeil, D. W. (2003). A brief behavioral activation treatment for depression. *Behavior Modification*, *27*, 458–469.

Hopko, D. R., Lejuez, C. W., Ruggiero, K., & Eifert, G. (2003). Contemporary behavioral activation treatments for depression: Procedures, principles and progress. *Clinical Psychology Review*, *23*, 699–717.

Horwitz, A., Wakefield, J. C., & Spitzer, R. L. (2007). *The loss of sadness: How psychiatry transformed normal sorrow into depressive disorder*. New York: Oxford University Press.

Iwata, B., Kahng, S., Wallace, M., & Lindberg, J. (2000). The functional analysis model of behavioral assessment. In J. Austin & J. E. Carr (Eds.), *Handbook of applied behavior analysis*. Reno, NV: Context Press.

Jacobson, N. S., Dobson, K. S., Truax, P. A., Addis, M. E., Koerner, K., Gollan, J. K., et al. (1996). A component analysis of cognitive behavioral treatment for depression. *Journal of Consulting and Clinical Psychology*, *64*, 295–304.

Jacobson, N., & Gortner, E. (2000). Can depression be de-medicalized in the 21st century: Scientific revolutions, counter-revolutions and the magnetic field of normal science. *Behaviour Research and Therapy*, *38*, 103–117.

Jakupcak, M., Roberts, L., Martell, C., Mulick, P., Michael, S., Reed, R., et al. (2006). A pilot study of behavioral activation for veterans with posttraumatic stress disorder. *Journal of Traumatic Stress*, *19*, 387–391.

Jonas, B., & Mussolino, M. (2000). Symptoms of depression as a prospective risk factor for stroke. *Psychosomatic Medicine*, *62*, 463–471.

Kanter, J. W., Baruch, D., & Gaynor, S. (2006). Acceptance and commitment therapy and behavioral activation for the treatment of depression: Description and comparison. *Behavior Analyst*, *29*, 161–185.

Kanter, J. W., Busch, A. M., Weeks, C. E., & Landes, S. J. (2008). The nature of clinical depression: Symptoms, syndromes, and behavior analysis. *The Behavior Analyst*, *31*, 1–21.

Kanter, J. W., Cautilli, J. D., Busch A. M., & Baruch, D. E. (2005). Toward a comprehensive functional analysis of depressive behavior: Five environmental factors and a possible sixth and seventh. *The Behavior Analyst Today*, *6*, 65–81.

Kanter, J. W., Manos, R. C., Busch, A. M., & Rusch, L. C. (2008).

Making behavioral activation more behavioral. *Behavior Modification, 32*, 780–803.

Kanter, J. W., Mulick, P. S., Busch, A. M., Berlin, K. S., & Martell, C. R. (2007) The Behavioral Activation for Depression Scale (BADS): Psychometric properties and factor structure. *Journal of Psychopathology and Behavioral Assessment, 29*, 191–202.

Kanter, J. W., Rusch, L. C., Busch, A. M., & Sedivy, S. K. (in press). Confirmatory factor analysis of the behavioral activation for depression scale (BADS) in a community sample with elevated depressive symptoms. *Journal of Psychopathology and Behavioral Assessment*.

Kanter, J. W., Weeks, C. E., Bonow, J. T., Landes, S. J., Callaghan, G. M., & Follette, W. C. (in press). Assessment and case conceptualization. In M. Tsai, R. J. Kohlenberg, J. W. Kanter, B. Kohlenberg, W. C. Follette, & G. M. Callaghan (Eds.), *A guide to functional analytic psychotherapy: Awareness, courage, love and behaviorism in the therapeutic relationship*. New York: Springer.

Kessler, R. C. (1997). The effects of stressful life events on depression. *Annual Review of Psychology, 48*, 191–214.

Kimbrough, R., Molock, S., & Walton, K. (1996). Perception of social support, acculturation, depression, and suicidal ideation among African American college students at predominantly black and predominantly white universities. *Journal of Negro Education, 65*, 295–307.

Klein, D., & Seligman, M. (1976). Reversal of performance deficits and perceptual deficits in learned helplessness and depression. *Journal of Abnormal Psychology, 85*, 11–26.

Kohlenberg, R. J., Kanter, J. W., Bolling, M. Y., Parker, C. R., & Tsai, M. (2002). Enhancing cognitive therapy for depression with functional analytic psychotherapy: Treatment guidelines and empirical findings. *Cognitive and Behavioral Practice, 9*, 213–229.

Kohlenberg, R. J., & Tsai, M. (1991). *Functional analytic psychotherapy: Creating intense and curative therapeutic relationships*. New York: Plenum Press.

Lejuez, C. W., Hopko, D. R., & Hopko, S. D. (2001). A brief behavioral activation treatment for depression: Treatment manual. *Behavior Modification, 25*, 255–286.

Lejuez, C. W., Hopko, D. R., & Hopko, S. D. (2002). *The brief Behavioral Activation Treatment for Depression (BATD): A comprehensive patient guide*. Boston: Pearson Custom Publishing.

Leventhal, A., & Martell, C. (2006). *The myth of depression as disease: Limitations and alternatives to drug treatment*. Westport, CT: Praeger Publishers/Greenwood Publishing Group.

Lewinsohn, P. (1974). A behavioral approach to depression. In R. J. Friedman & M. M. Katz (Eds.), *Psychology of depression: Contemporary theory and research*. Oxford, England: John Wiley & Sons.

Lewinsohn, P. M., Antonuccio, D. O., Steinmetz-Breckenridge, J., & Teri, L. (1984). *The coping with depression course*. Eugene, OR: Castalia Press.

Lewinsohn, P. M., Muñoz, R. F., Youngren, M. A., & Zeiss, A. M. (1978). *Control your depression*. New York: Prentice Hall.

Lincoln, K. D., Chatters, L. M., & Taylor, R. J. (2005). Social support, traumatic events, and depressive symptoms among African Americans. *Journal of Marriage and Family, 67*, 754–766.

Linehan, M. (1993). *Cognitive-behavioral treatment of borderline personality disorder*. New York: Guilford Press.

Longmore, R., & Worrell, M. (2007). Do we need to challenge thoughts in cognitive behavior therapy? *Clinical Psychology Review, 27*, 173–187.

Martell, C. R., Addis, M. E., & Jacobson, N. S. (2001). *Depression in context: Strategies for guided action*. New York: Norton.

Masedo, A., & Esteve, M. (2007). Effects of suppression, acceptance and spontaneous coping on pain tolerance, pain intensity and distress. *Behaviour Research and Therapy, 45*, 199–209.

McCullough, J. P. (2000). *Treatment for chronic depression: Cognitive Behavioral Analysis System of Psychotherapy*. New York: Guilford.

Melin, L., Andersson, B., & Götestam, K. (1976). Contingency management in a methadone maintenance treatment program. *Addictive Behaviors, 1*, 151–158.

Miller, D., Malmstrom, T., Joshi, S., Andresen, E., Morley, J., & Wolinsky, F. (2004). Clinically relevant levels of depressive symptoms in community-dwelling middle-aged African Americans. *Journal of the American Geriatrics Society, 52*, 741–748.

Mulick, P., & Naugle, A. (2004). Behavioral activation for comorbid PTSD and major depression: A case study. *Cognitive and Behavioral Practice, 11*, 378–387.

Nezu, A. M., Nezu, C. M., & Perri, M. G. (1989). *Problem-solving therapy for depression: Theory, research, and clinical guidelines*. New York: Wiley.

Overmier, J., & Seligman, M. (1967). Effects of inescapable shock upon subsequent escape and avoidance responding. *Journal of Comparative and Physiological Psychology, 63*, 28–33.

Porter, J., Spates, C., & Smitham, S. (2004). Behavioral activation group therapy in public mental health settings: A pilot investigation. *Professional Psychology: Research and Practice, 35*, 297–301.

Ramnerö, J., & Törneke, N. (2008). *ABCs of human behavior: Behavioral principles for the practicing clinician*. Reno, NV: Context Press.

Riolo, S. A., Nguyen, T., Greden, J. F., & King, C. A. (2005). Prevolence of depression by race/ethnicity: Findings from the National Health and Nutrition Examination Survey III. *American Journal of Public Health, 95*, 998–1000.

Roth, S., & Kubal, L. (1975). Effects of noncontingent reinforcement on tasks of differing importance: Facilitation and learned helplessness. *Journal of Personality and Social Psychology, 32*, 680–691.

Rusch, L. C., Kanter, J. W., & Brondino, M. J. (in press). A comparison of the behavioral and biomedical models of stigma reduction for depression with a non-clinical undergraduate sample. *The Journal of Nervous and Mental Disease*.

Santiago-Rivera, A., Arredondo, P., & Gallardo-Cooper, M. (2002). *Counseling Latinos and la familia: A practical guide*. Thousand Oaks, CA: Sage.

Santiago-Rivera, A., Kanter, J. W., Benson, G., DeRose, T., Illes, R., & Reyes, W. (in press). Behavioral activation treatment approach for Latinos with depression. *Psychotherapy: Theory, Research, Practice, Training*.

Sergin, C. (2003). Social skills training. In W. O'Donohue, J. E. Fisher, & S. C. Hayes (Eds.), *Cognitive behavior therapy: Applying empirically supported techniques in your practice*. Hoboken, NJ: John Wiley & Sons, Inc.

Simons, A. D., Garfield, S. L., & Murphy, G. E. (1984). The process of change in cognitive therapy and pharmacotherapy for depression: Changes in mood and cognition. *Archives of General Psychiatry, 41*, 45–51.

Skinner, B. F. (1953). *Science and human behavior*. Oxford, England: Macmillan.

Skinner, B. F. (1974). *About behaviorism*. New York: Vintage Books.

Tsai, M., Kohlenberg, R. J., Kanter, J. W., Kohlenberg, B., Follette, W. C., & Callaghan, G. M. (Eds.) (2008). *A guide to functional analytic psychotherapy: Awareness, courage, love, and behaviorism in the therapeutic relationship*. New York: Springer.

Valenstein, E. S. (1988). *Blaming the brain: The truth about drugs and mental health*. New York: The Free Press.

Veale, D. (2008). Behavioural activation for depression. *Advances in Psychiatric Treatment, 14*, 29–36.

Wegner, D., & Zanakos, S. I. (1994). Chronic thought suppression. *Journal of Personality, 62*, 615–640.

Wells, A. (2004). Metacognitive therapy: Elements of mental control in understanding and treating generalized anxiety disorder and post-traumatic stress disorder. *Contemporary cognitive therapy: Theory, research, and practice* (pp. 184–205). New York: Guilford Press.

Wilson, K. G., Sandoz, E. K., Kitchens, J., & Roberts, M. E. (2008). *The Valued Living Questionnaire: Defining and measuring valued action within a behavioral framework*. Manuscript submitted for publication.

Woods, D. W., & Kanter, J. W. (Eds.) (2007). *Understanding behavior Disorders: A contemporary behavioral perspective*. Reno, NV: Context Press.

Zeiss, A., Lewinsohn, P., & Muñoz, R. (1979). Nonspecific improvement effects in depression using interpersonal skills training, pleasant activity schedules, or cognitive training. *Journal of Consulting and Clinical Psychology*, *47*, 427–439.

Author index

177

Subject index